ST ~ EDUCATION LI

You Can *Still*
Change the World

You Can *Still* Change the World

RICHARD ARMSTRONG

and EDWARD WAKIN

1817

Published in San Francisco by

HARPER & ROW, PUBLISHERS

New York, Hagerstown, San Francisco, London

Grateful acknowledgment is made to Little, Brown and Co. for permisson to reprint a portion of "Election Day is a Holiday" from *Many Long Years Ago* by Ogden Nash, copyright © 1932 by Ogden Nash. British copyright rights reprinted by permission of Curtis Brown, Ltd.

FIRST EDITION

Designed by Jim Mennick

Library of Congress Cataloging in Publication Data
Armstrong, Richard G
  YOU CAN STILL CHANGE THE WORLD.

  1. Change (Psychology) 2. Social change.
3. Success. I. Wakin, Edward, joint author.
II. Title.
BF637.C4A75   1978   158'.1   77–6160
ISBN 06–060304–6
ISBN 06–060302–x pbk.

Contents

Foreword

It is one thing to make a living. It is quite another to make a life. In *You Can* Still *Change the World* authors Armstrong and Wakin offer practical wisdom, specific examples, pointed questions, and helpful tips to enable you to take another look at *your* world and *the* world.

This book takes seriously the question "What can I do?" and answers it simply and unpretentiously with the word "Something." Because you are unique and unrepeatable. Because your family relationships affect the way you live. Because your attitude toward your own ability and your work colors your entire existence. Because you are a leader, whether you recognize it or not. Because it is up to you to decide whether and how to involve yourself in the compelling issues that determine the course of our nation and world. Because you are one person and you can make a difference.

This is a book you can read for information; it is packed with facts and statistics that can make you better informed. It is a book you can turn to for inspiration and encouragement when the fire of enthusiasm burns low. It is a book you can read for enjoyment. The authors have shaped their message with an eye to holding your attention.

It is above all a book of faith, hope, and love. It believes in the power of one person and in the God who created all people. It is hopeful about the potentialities of human freedom to make sound and far-reaching decisions. And it is a book of love—not of the sentimental kind that falls away under adversity, but of the kind that the apostle Paul described and that Jesus lived.

So, learn from it. Draw strength from it. Enjoy it. And try to live by it. *You Can* Still *Change the World* was written for you. As the authors say, it is incomplete, because the future chapters are to be written, not on paper, but in the lives of the flesh and blood people who believe they can make a difference, and then go out and do it.

THEODORE M. HESBURGH, C.S.C.
President, University of Notre Dame

Introduction

Do you believe you can still change the world? Chances are you do. Or at least you hope it's true. Otherwise, you wouldn't even have picked up this book.

Most of us want to believe that the world can be changed, and we would like to think we can help change it. One Christopher friend put it succinctly: "How I wish to add my grain of sand to the transformation of the world!"

Don't we all? *You Can* Still *Change the World* will try to confirm your belief that this is possible and will suggest ways in which you can make a start right now.

ONE MAN'S VISION

James Keller, a Maryknoll missioner, started the Christopher movement in 1945. He was convinced that every person of good will is—or can be—a missionary in the broadest sense of that word. He was constantly telling anyone who would listen: "You have a unique role to play in God's plan. He wants to transmit some of his truth and love through you. And if you don't transmit your share, who will?"

The first vehicle for getting across that fundamental Christopher idea was *Christopher News Notes.* This brief newsletter—about the length of a feature magazine article—started with a circulation of forty-five thousand. Within two years, circulation had doubled. Within a decade, it had nearly topped the million mark.

YOU CAN CHANGE THE WORLD

"Although the *News Notes* were effective and I certainly intended to continue with them," Father Keller later wrote, "I knew that after the bulletins had been read, they could easily be lost, misplaced, or thrown away. So I went to work on a book that incorporated the ideas expressed in the *Notes.*"

That book was *You Can Change the World,* published in 1948 by Longmans Green. It tapped the idealism and hope for the future many people were feeling in the wake of the Second World War. It gave a constructive focus to the fear of another conflagration that characterized the cold war era. It told a wide range of readers that they could renew government, education, labor-management relations, literature, and the creative side of entertainment. And it stimulated a surprising number of men and women to do just that.

Over the years more than two hundred fifty thousand hardbound and paperback copies reached readers with the simple Christopher message of constructive individual action in the public interest. The Christopher movement became a national presence in both print and electronic media.

CHANGING TIMES

No one needs to be told that the world has changed since 1948. The Christophers has changed over the decades too. Father Keller retired in 1969. The Christophers, under the directorship of Richard Armstrong, was faced with the challenge of transforming a movement that had been essentially the extension of one man's charisma into a professionally-managed, solidly-based organization. At the same time, the message—"There's Nobody Like You" and "You Can Make a Difference"—had to be refined to meet the needs of a world hurtling toward the twenty-first century.

Christopher News Notes, special publications, and television programs focused increasingly on tough issues—prison reform, world hunger, drug abuse, threatened families, the needs of handicapped persons. We took more than one look at questions of global justice and peace. We tried to find in each of these issues—and in the more personal questions such as faith, prayer, self-esteem—a continuing affirmation of our belief that each person is sacred and special and that each is meant to help renew the face of the earth.

Gradually, the need Father Keller had felt in 1948 resurfaced: *News Notes* and "Christopher Closeup," our weekly television show, were excellent means, but they were transitory. Once again the Christopher message had to be encapsulated in a single volume that would be easy to get at, easy to understand, and easy to use. In 1948, James Keller felt the need to put between bound covers the message, "You Can Change the World." Now we feel the same drive to tell all we can reach, "You Can *Still* Change the World."

The Peace Corps, the civil rights movement, consumerism and ecological concern, Watergate, and other events in recent history have demonstrated just how much individuals can achieve with leadership, singleness of vision, and persistence. Our inner cities, the plight of the elderly and the urban and the rural poor, and the continuing arms race, among other crying needs, show how far we have to go.

A PERENNIAL MESSAGE

You Can Still *Change the World* is an affirmation by The Christophers, now two years into our fourth decade, that James Keller's vision still lives. It is an attempt to keep that vision alive and active. And it is a request to men and women everywhere who have been lighting candles in the darkness to, as Father Keller used to say, "keep on keeping on."

The world we all long for may not come quickly or easily, but faith tells us that it will surely come. If we choose, we can speed its arrival.

If he were alive today, James Keller would say, "Yes, indeed, you can still change the world." I hope this book will help you see why—and how.

WILLIAM J. WILSON
Editor, Christopher Publications

‹ 1 ›

There's Nobody Like You

No one like you has ever lived before, and there will never again be someone quite like you. You, like every living person, are unprecedented—unique, special, unrepeatable.

All of us are here in the face of breathtaking genetic odds. We are present and accounted for among the infinite alternatives that might be present in our place in this world at this time.

We have emerged as God's special handiwork, with a special array of traits, characteristics, and qualities. Background and experiences come together in a once-in-forever way for each human being.

God has not trifled. Divine handiwork does not cut corners in nature. Blessed individuality shines from each living person's eyes and throbs through each person's body. Touch a table with your fingertips, examine a tree with your eyes, listen for the sounds of a loved one, feel your feet upon the ground.

Or close your eyes and stop a moment to concentrate on your breathing. Try to clear your mind of any thoughts. Count each time you exhale, going from one to ten. Repeat this a few times. You are getting in touch with the universe that is you, registering your existence.

All of us share a magnificent, one-time-only opportunity by

existing in God's universe. Do not waste the opportunity to live in the only meaningful and satisfying way: *You shall love your neighbor as yourself.*

Begin with your individuality. Accept who you are and develop a proper love of self. In *On Becoming a Person,* psychologist Carl Rogers says of himself, "I find I am more effective when I can listen acceptantly to myself, and can be myself." God singles out love of self as the guide for love of others; yet many people go through life without learning to accept themselves.

Each person needs to believe he or she is unique. Each needs to be reminded that this is a fact. Each person wants to mean something to other people and to God. Each wants to do things in life that can make a difference. Each flourishes when reminded of the difference he or she can make.

Look around. The world is filled with people who are making a difference without fanfare or publicity. Their friends know them, and we at The Christophers get to know many of them through letters that arrive every day at the Christopher Center at 12 East 48th Street in New York City. A few examples from a steady stream of mail show how individual men and women are changing their world for the better:

"I am a mother of six children. I work part time as a nurse in a pediatric unit. I truly believe that if I do my work with love it will be obvious to others and will stimulate them to do the same. I pray for God to teach me to love so deeply that no task is too difficult for me. I really love and comfort the little ones in my care. Some of these children are neglected or ill-treated at home. I hope that through my care they can get a hint of the love that is so necessary for their development."

"Since I was a child in Philadelphia after World War II, your theme has been an inspiration to me. I have been an M.S. patient for the past ten years, and I am presently trying to help other 'handicapped' people here in Puerto Rico."

"I am a township manager and am therefore particularly interested in your number one aim: raising the standards of government. I will continue to try to do that, always starting here, with me, in my office."

"I am teaching reading to inmates of a maximum security prison. It is for sixteen- to twenty-eight-year-olds. . . . I have them for one hour a day for three to six months average, and they cover the equivalent of one to five years of schoolwork in that time. I work hard and so do they. Some have gone to college. At least half have changed their lives somewhat because I have made them aware of their potential and have given them confidence and self-esteem. . . . Most of my students have the potential of a very fine character. I love them because they are children of God."

"I am eighty-two with only one eye—and that has a cataract. The doctor doesn't understand how I see through it, but doesn't recommend removing it. My hearing is poor, have a hearing aid. My balance not good, my knees are bad—but I am perfectly happy with what God does for me. There is nothing I really want except to retain enough sight so I can keep on doing the work. Some people call it work, I consider it play. I am chairman of a Beano group. So many older people have no recreation, and they love to get together and enjoy an afternoon of Beano. Low prices, good prizes, refreshments. I do the calling. . . . I believe the Lord can heal, all I ask is to be able to do as I am now. I have wonderful neighbors, and five children with families. I don't want to live with them as long as I can be independent. I have to use a glass to read; so please excuse mistakes and keep up your wonderful work!"

It is characteristic of such letters that the writers graciously extend praise, when it is they who deserve the praise. But they don't want acclaim for what they do. The doing is their reward. They are, as the late Rabbi Abraham Heschel would put it, sancti-

fying time, the precious here-and-now of their earthly existence
—"The chief end of man is to sanctify time. All it takes to sanctify
time is God, a soul and a moment. And the three are always
here."

The process of sanctifying time is as old as human faith and
as fresh as its latest formulation. The message is new every time
it is heard and acted upon. So easily remembered yet so easily
forgotten, so matter-of-fact yet so miraculous, so ordinary yet so
special, the process is epitomized by the two basic ideas which
The Christophers has worked to spread:

There's nobody like you.
You can make a difference.

Based on the Judeo-Christian concept of service to God and
all humanity, the Christopher message is addressed to people of
all faiths and of no particular faith. It is an invitation to participate
in a process that involves:

Love of others built on healthy self-love.
Self-awareness.
Action in the here and now.

Loving yourself means accepting what you are. You recognize what you have been given, and you don't try to justify yourself by first seeking the applause of others.

If you love yourself, you realize your limitations, without
surrendering to them. You don't use your limitations as an excuse for not acting nor do you put down yourself for being
inferior. You don't settle for less because you don't feel like less.
You just get on with the job at hand without playing superman
or superwoman or sulking in the corner as a reject.

If you love yourself, you accept contradictions and frustrations without being devastated. These are calls to service, not
excuses for giving in. They are opportunities to recognize the
needs of others when they are different from yours, to realize that
there are different strokes for different folks.

If you love yourself, you pay attention to others, listen to their problems, try to help them without wondering "What's in it for me?" You are too broad-minded to envy, too clearsighted to hate, too interested in others to indulge in self-pity.

If you love yourself, you will have a sense of humor. You will not be silly and frivolous or chuckle bitterly at the mishaps of others, but you will laugh, sometimes aloud, at the joy and mystery of life. You will revel in the part you play in it.

Loving yourself is a faint reflection of the eternal mystery of God, a gift to be shared, a treasure that grows by being spent, a dynamism that imparts meaning and purpose to life.

When you love yourself, you inevitably realize that you are joined to others in the common bond of humanity. You have the power to relate to others in a warm, loving manner. You feel the need, as well as the responsibility, to express concern and take constructive action in the world around you—neighborhood and school, community and church, state and nation.

To develop and maintain a perspective on the way you live out your love of self and others, self-awareness is necessary. Examine yourself and your life. An ancient piece of advice by Plato is as current as ever: "The life which is unexamined is not worth living." Moments of silence and reflection are essential. Otherwise, you will be swept along by the complexity of things and run the danger of losing yourself in the world.

Here are some questions to ask in figuring out where you personally stand. But don't only raise them by yourself; also get feedback from people you trust and respect.

Am I convinced of my personal worth?

Do I respect the integrity of others?

Am I so involved in material things that I ignore life's really important dimensions of being myself and being in close touch with others?

What turns me on? People or things? Do I depend mainly on things for satisfaction?

Do I believe there is a special and unique contribution that only I can make toward a better world?

Am I willing to take risks and encounter difficulties in putting my constructive ideas to work?

Do I admire people who help others? Or do I admire those who have power over others?

How do I define success? As money, power, fame? Or as a fulfillment of myself by using talents for and with others, by sharing myself and my love?

Do I trust God enough to do my best and leave the results with him?

Take stock of what God has given you; find out what is distinctively you. Identify your strengths and weaknesses, your accomplishments and your shortcomings. Look upon yourself as an unfinished product that is continuously in process—for the whole of your life. You are doing the finishing yourself, and you can never stop. "We are always involved, like it or not," writer Joan Ulanov points out, "in the suspenseful and difficult process of becoming something neither we nor anyone else ever was before."

In discovering and expressing your individuality, be a doer, one of the three kinds of people described by the late Nicholas Murray Butler, former president of Columbia University. *Doers* are the few people who make things happen. *Onlookers* are the many who watch things happen. The *uninterested* are the large majority who have no idea of what is happening.

Your life becomes more interesting when you become a doer; so do you as an individual. Your special, unrepeatable life moves toward greater fulfillment and satisfaction. You personally carry on a perpetual exploration of who you are, for in *doing,* you discover your uniqueness. Your actions speak louder and clearer than anything else in proclaiming who you are.

By your actions you break through the walls that you build around yourself and that others build around themselves. By your actions, you shall know your goals and work toward them. You shall be both free and responsible. Your life takes on meaning as actions develop your potential and as you move toward goals. Without goals, life becomes empty. As the essayist Montaigne pointed out: "No wind favors him who has no destined port."

The purpose of life is not merely to be yourself. It must be —and is—something bigger. The life worth living testifies to the oneness of humankind, to the bond that unites each person who ever lived, lives, or will live, to the unfolding possibilities of the human adventure. You—specifically you—have a unique role to play in unfolding human possibilities.

This means facing the reality that your life is literally in your own hands. The Lord provides the "makings" of a reasonably full, happy existence, but each individual needs to discover and develop these elements. Your life is what you make of it—by *doing.* The word *satisfaction* expresses this message in its composition: the Latin *satis* means "enough"; *facere* means "to make or to do."

There is no need for anyone to lead a life of gnawing dissatisfaction. However great or limited your resources, education, or circumstances, you have a unique contribution of self to make. That self is under your control, and what you do with it is what counts. Each person is needed by others as much as the individual needs others. Cardinal John Henry Newman eloquently underlined this theme:

> God has created me to do Him
> some definite service;
> He has committed some work to me
> which he has not committed to another.
> I have my mission . . .
> I am a link in a chain,
> a bond of connection between persons.
> He has not created me for naught.
> I shall do good. I shall do His work.
> I shall be an angel of peace,
> a preacher of truth in my own place

while not intending it—
if I do but keep His commandments.

The time to apply the twofold commandment of love is now;
the place is here. Start where you are—in your family, job, school,
neighborhood, community. If you fail to develop the divine knack
of showing a reasonable concern for people in their own little
worlds, then you are unlikely to develop a meaningful capacity
for relating to the problems of humankind.

Each June when commencement ceremonies take place at
schools throughout the country, this challenging summons of
meaningful service is directed toward graduates. But actually
every minute is a commencement, and you are the one gradua-
ting. It would be a mistake to think of graduation only as a
celebration for the young. No one reminds the world of this any
better than do older people.

At eighty-seven, psychiatrist and author Dr. Olga Knopf described what it is like to be approaching ninety. "There is real
satisfaction in old age—if you will take pride in what you still can
do." Her formula is exemplified in different ways by different
people.

At eighty-two, Samuel Greene of New Jersey was living
on the side of a mountain in Guatemala, helping Indian com-
munities. He took up that career after "retiring" at age sixty-
eight.

At eighty-eight, David Cunningham, a retired janitor, was
well known throughout Columbus, Ohio, for his work with young
people.

At eighty-four, a nursing home patient in Pueblo, Colorado,
got out of his wheelchair and became a full-time gardener, pro-
viding fellow patients with a variety of fresh vegetables.

At eighty-nine, Stella Turner of Atlanta, Georgia, was busy
with her own ceramics business. She switched to ceramics at
eighty after a career as a practical nurse that began at sixty.

At seventy-two, Dr. Eugene Balthazar of Aurora, Illinois, was
running a free clinic that he started with his savings.

At ninety-five, Welthy Honsinger Fisher of Connecticut "slowed down" to round-the-world lecturing and fundraising for her literacy campaign in India.

Dr. Knopf's advice to older people applies to everyone: "If you look forward, the world is yours." The world is at your doorstep whether you are a nine-year-old starting a magazine to tell other youngsters about children in poor countries (and earning twenty-five dollars monthly for a children's hospital in Africa) or a "happy bus driver" in Hartford, Connecticut, or a free veterinarian in Chicago or a nineteen-year-old protector of the osprey on Long Island Sound or a twelve-year-old city commissioner in San Anselmo, California.

People are making a difference at every age and station in life: the bus driver turned his suburban express trip into a happy hour of sing-alongs and socializing; the veterinarian gave his services away to poor children with pets; the college student stemmed the decline in the large fish hawks called osprey by bringing in eggs uncontaminated by DDT; the young girl convinced a city council that children needed a say in how parks are run.

Examples never stop, and The Christophers can only call attention to some of them in our regular newspaper column, "What One Person Can Do." Each example demonstrates the stream of hope flowing from the faith that the world makes sense and that individual human beings matter. The hope is contagious. It is serious too, but not gloomy, for hope does not grimace or grind teeth. Realistic hope looks to the present instead of staring into a rear-view mirror. Meaningful hope looks for ways to express itself in action. This theme is expressed in the Christopher "Prayer to Live in the Present":

> God
> I spend so much time reliving yesterday
> or anticipating tomorrow
> that I lose sight of the only time
> that is really mine—the present.

Remind me that the past—with its successes
and failures—is over.
I can make amends where I have hurt others
or let them down
but I can't undo what has been done.
The future is yet to be
and eagerness or apprehension
will not hasten it—or postpone it.
You give me today, one minute at a time.
That's all I have—all I ever will.
Give me the faith that knows that each moment
contains exactly what is best for me.
Give me the hope that trusts You enough to
forget past sins and future trials.
Give me the love that makes each minute of
life an anticipation of eternity with You.
Amen.

This brings us back to the commandment that encompasses all commandments—love your neighbor as yourself. Focus on the precious, irretrievable ingredient of time, the stuff of which life is made. Make your time count. Each minute, day, year is given you only once; then it is gone forever. "Killing time" is a form of murder, for it destroys the stuff of life. Using time to be in touch with yourself and with others is to treat that precious commodity with the reverence it deserves. Thus do you sanctify the time of your life.

To do so you must reach out, not stay confined inside yourself. It helps to remember that you cannot repeat the Lord's Prayer and even once say *I* or *my*. We are called to place in circulation the share of love that God sends to humankind through each person. To withhold that love is to cheat those for whom it was intended. Multiply this small failure to "deliver" by many millions, and a staggering picture of desolation emerges. Such omissions cast a dark shadow over the world.

By contrast, each individual who keeps self-interest in its

proper place for the common good of all serves both self and others. That is the life-serving challenge: To work toward goals that express love of self as the criterion for love of others. You thereby fulfill others and are fulfilled. To repeat: What is important is *doing*. Erich Fromm, at seventy-six still writing and still trying to arouse humankind to its potential, cited an admonition from the Talmud, the record of Jewish canon and civil law: "It is not up to you to finish the task, but you have no right to withhold."

The challenge of the Christopher motto is as bright and meaningful as ever. Constantly reaffirmed in the human drama, it speaks to every individual: *Better to light one candle than to curse the darkness.*

‹ 2 ›

The Challenge of Loving

We all experience the greatest challenge of loving in family life —as son or daughter, husband or wife, father or mother. Many people experience love in all three roles.

Throughout human history, the family has been *the* school of love and *the* laboratory for personal closeness. It seems beyond imagination, no matter what the future brings, that the family will ever go out of business. For all the criticisms heaped upon family life in the modern world, it remains the primary agency in which persons learn to care for one another. A perceptive commentator, Rosemary Haughton, points out that "the purpose of a family is for the formation of people who are able to love."

Past, present, and future are represented in the three family roles that most men and women play in their lifetimes. Now a fourth dimension has been added: middle-aged sons and daughters relating to aging parents as life expectancy increases.

The most intimate of all relations is, of course, between husband and wife, and this is the relationship that is freely chosen. A lifetime decision is made with the two words *I do*. One couple commented wryly on celebrating their twelfth wedding anniversary: "If we'd had any real idea what those two words meant, we probably never would have had the courage to say them!"

Marriage has been compared to the story of two porcupines who found themselves stranded on a cold winter night and tried to keep warm by huddling together. When they came too close and crowded each other, they hurt each other with their quills, and when they moved apart, they were cold. What they had to find was the distance at which they could adjust to each other's quills while still staying close enough to keep warm.

Marriage, as the experts point out, is fulfilling when each partner masters the art of closeness without destroying the integrity of the other. Each must take responsibility for himself or herself in and out of the relationship. In marriage one plus one equals two together, as in arithmetic, not a merger into one. "The goal in marriage," Robert Dodds has written, "is not to think alike, but to think together."

The greatness of a marriage relationship comes from the opportunity for each partner to grow and benefit from the constructive feedback of an equal. In marriage we share our life with someone who has common experiences, someone who is "on our side," someone who has chosen us and whom we have chosen. Personal feedback in marriage enables us to learn a great deal about ourselves and thereby helps fulfill us as human beings.

Marriage is certainly not the only relationship that can provide all this. Family and friends also fill such a role. But no other relationship is set up the way marriage is—emotionally, psychologically, culturally, socially, and legally. Society has stacked the cards in favor of marriage being *the* special relationship in life, and obviously the large majority of men and women ask to be dealt in.

The words *I do* mean that two people have embarked on a relationship that involves:

- a mutually enriching experience
- an acceptance of the arduous challenge of personal development
- a continuing gift of self

- an atmosphere of love and strength for the nurturing of new life
- a reflection in some mysterious manner of the unity God desires for his world.

But marriage does not exist in a fairyland. It is lived out in an environment that takes its toll, as is evident from the rising divorce rate: almost one million marriages a year self-destruct. What everyone must do to develop and maintain a satisfying marriage applies to all relationships, but marriage is the best example of what a close, loving relationship demands.

To succeed in any relationship you must know who you are and what your values, needs, and goals are. You have to appreciate the fact that "There's Nobody Like You" and bring this awareness to the relationship. Many couples marry without sharing and discussing each other's basic feelings, ideals, and expectations. Some even unrealistically hope that marriage will "change" the other person or supply from the outside what must be supplied from within. Even when marriages begin without open and honest sharing, they can get on the right track with joint effort (and sometimes professional assistance).

Within marriage, personality clashes develop when one wants to "get" more than he or she is willing to "give" to meet the needs of a partner. Specific problems arise from the inability or refusal to discuss matters of common concern . . . disagreements on having and raising children . . . conflicts involving in-laws . . . too little money or mismanagement of finances . . . lack of privacy or inadequate housing . . . career demands by husband and/or wife . . . neglect of or overpreoccupation with children . . . religious differences or indifference . . . resistance to change.

External pressures are created by proponents of ideas and attitudes that tend to discredit Judeo-Christian values. Other pressures come from the excessive demands of friends, relatives, and neighbors; from the commercial exploitation of sex and distortions of its place in marriage; and from the discouraging influence of couples whose marriages are in crisis. Amidst such pressures, couples may feel a lack of adequate support and practical assistance from traditional community and religious sources.

Couples must work frankly and prayerfully in the face of these outside forces. They must reaffirm the stability of their home as a center of life and warmth that extends to the community, nation, and world. Within the marriage, each partner has to take personal responsibility. It takes two to make a marriage succeed.

When a woman who had been married fifty years was asked if she were ever tempted to divorce her husband, she replied jokingly: "Divorce—never! But murder—many times!" She was expressing the determination that is needed to make a marriage work, an acceptance of the reality that there will be hard times, problems, misunderstandings, arguments, and even outright conflict. Living up to—rather than walking away from—the demands of a close relationship can make married life one of the most rewarding human experiences.

When quarrels occur, the following steps, suggested by Dr. Edward Litin of the Mayo Clinic, are helpful:

Seek a settlement or compromise.
Forget the dispute afterwards.
Limit yourselves to the subject under discussion.
Refrain from words that will be regretted later.
Conclude by agreeing on a course of action.

Another step can be added: be willing to apologize. "Do not let the sun go down on your anger" (Eph. 4:26, RSV).

By keeping lines of communication open, two people in a relationship can anticipate crises and deal with them before they explode. Living together gives husband and wife many possibilities for close contact if they seek and use them. Instead of looking for things to do separately, they should try to find things they both like to do and do them together.

This can mean rearranging schedules. It can mean doing things around the house together, planning joint recreation, and using mealtime as an opportunity to share each other as well as food. It can mean using the time spent driving a husband to the train station or preparing dinner as occasions for personal interchange.

Dr. Philip Guerin, a family therapist in New Rochelle, New York, suggests that couples try a little experiment to judge how well they are keeping in close touch with each other. (It works just as well with any two people—parent and child, two friends, whatever.) Go out to dinner alone. Choose a restaurant where the service is particularly slow and where each course takes time. Notice what happens to your conversation.

What do you talk about? The weather? The day's news? The decor in the restaurant? What color to paint the living room? Which car to buy? Where to go on vacation? Why the phone bill is running so high? Where? How much? Now? Later? Sooner? One *thing* after another. If you find that the conversation *never* gets personal, never goes into feelings and attitudes toward life and love, never gets into what is going on inside each person, then you have an indication that the relationship does not include the stuff of which relationships are made: the personal.

But one person is not going to get personal with another unless he or she is convinced the other listens. When someone finishes your sentences for you or wants to do all the talking, then you and he or she are not on the same wavelength. You are traveling parallel lines that only meet in infinity. One technique to see how well you listen is to see if you can repeat what has just been said. You must repeat what the speaker has said to the speaker's satisfaction before talking yourself. This produces startling results!

An increasingly popular method for helping couples renew their relationship is a program called "Marriage Encounter." Couples go away for a uniquely structured weekend during which they discover new techniques for communication, evaluate their relationship, and generally open themselves to each other as never before.

Together they explore such topics as the following:

I—What are my strong points as a person? What is my main defect as a mate?

We—What are the things we like most (least) about each other? Do we see and accept each other as we really are? What most unites (separates) us?

Children—What do we think about each child? Where do we agree (disagree) about each one of them? Do they lack confidence in us? Are they trained in freedom and in love?

God—What does God expect from us now? What draws us closer to him and to each other?

Dr. Guerin says that the goal in marriage is to have two well-defined *selves* make a well-defined *we.* Each retains his or her identity in sharing the self. In the process, "one partner cannot make the other happy." Blaming does not work. Don't blame someone else for your problems or take the blame for someone else's problems. Clearly, you can and should help the other person, but you cannot live someone else's life, even if that person is your spouse, your parent, or your child.

Many people carry unnecessary guilt over the feelings of others. It is easy to help others escape their responsibilities or to cooperate as they avoid facing themselves. It is tempting to do the same with yourself, blaming parents, children, the boss, the neighbor, or your partner. As Shakespeare noted, the trouble is not with our stars, but with ourselves.

Basically, all personal relationships center on feelings; what two people in a relationship do is share them. It's not easy, but that sharing brings two persons together. As in all important things, actions speak louder than words: how each treats the other. That is the practical way in which the family is "a school of love." So when someone says he or she is "touched," the meaning is clear enough: you have affected his or her feelings, gotten through to emotions, made conscious contact.

Touching also needs to be taken literally, as author and anthropologist Ashley Montagu has pointed out in *Touching*, his study of tactile experience. He refers to "the mind of the skin" and points out that the skin is not simply a covering for the body. It is a sense organ that provides experiences which are vital to the development of the young and important to everyone for a life-time. Touching is a powerful way to make contact, whether cud-dling an infant, kissing affectionately, or holding the hand of an elderly person.

Montagu's advice applies to personal relationships: "It is not words so much as acts communicating affection and involvement that children and, indeed, adults require." So, by all means, *please do touch.* Show affection in countless ways in all relationships. The most intimate physical expression of love is sexual intercourse between husband and wife, but intercourse is only part of a whole range of contacts that speak of love. Holding hands, a gentle arm on the shoulders, sitting next to each other—all signify closeness.

Children are particularly sensitive to the way adults treat each other. With their incredible antennae, children immediately sense the meaning of a touch. They don't miss an emotional clue, whether it passes between father and mother or parent and child. A touch that conveys positive feelings is louder than a shout to a child; the opposite, shriller than a scream. No sermons, no high-decibel protestations come close to the lesson of love taught by touching.

The truth of the family matter is that adults need to under-stand their experiences as children in order to understand them-selves, and to understand their children, parents need to under-stand themselves. After all, children aren't very different from the parents who bore them, reared them, and provided the primary school of love and closeness. The foundation for growing up is laid in the family.

A revealing flashback to your own childhood is the family

photo album. You will be surprised what turns up when you leaf through pages of old pictures, what you recall and what the other members of the family, particularly your parents, can point out. Ask a few questions as you look: Who was doing *what, when?* Who is in the pictures? Who is left out? Are people touching physically? Who is close to whom? What kind of feelings does the picture stir up? What impression do the people in the picture give you? What is the mood of the picture, of the people in it?

A trip through the family album works as well with your present family as it does with your own childhood. Pictures are clues to help you work out questions about what is happening between the people in the pictures. Psychologist Robert U. Akeret uses family photos in treating patients, as do an increasing number of therapists. "Photographs have a special language of their own, and *all* photographs tell some kind of story beyond the purely visual record," Dr. Akeret points out in *Photoanalysis.* He states that "like dreams, body language, slips of the tongue, and handwriting, photographs reveal significant aspects of individuals and are lasting records of our lives and deeds."

A look at yourself today in a family picture may remind you that you are doing what was done to you. How do you feel about that? Is that the way you want to deal with others, with your spouse, with your own children? Can you recall what it was like to be a child? How much you wanted to be understood and appreciated?

The age of television may have replaced Saturday at the movies or the Lone Ranger on radio, but children basically still want the same things. They want your love, which can be shown so wonderfully by your actions. When a group of boys and girls between eight and twelve years of age were asked how parents should act toward their children, there were no surprises, but there were some wonderful reminders:

Treat all children with equal affection.
Never lie to a child.

There should be comradeship between grownups and children.

Always answer questions. Never say, "Don't bother me now."

Don't blame or punish a child in the presence of the children next door.

Concentrate on a child's good points, not on his or her failings.

Be constant in mood and affection.

When youngsters were asked to set down "What Every Adult Should Know about Children," time and again they asked to be regarded as persons and to have their feelings respected:

"I think every adult should know that children are individuals."

"The most important thing that adults should know is that kids need love and help. Kids need them because if they don't have love or help, they could turn out wrong. Adults should know that kids are individuals and human beings."

"I think all adults should know our true feelings. They should know what our reactions are toward their demands."

"I think every adult should know that kids have feelings too and that adults should take their feelings seriously."

"Adults know other feelings about people. But if they stayed around children, they could find out that we have the same feelings."

"I think every adult should know that children try their best."

"Before an adult starts to learn about kids in general, I believe the adult should understand that all kids are different. If they want to know about kids, I believe they should learn about each one individually."*

*These comments were published in Edward Wakin, *The Battle for Childhood* (St. Meinrad, Ind.: Abbey Press, 1973).

Insistence that a child live up to some distant and abstract ideal does an injustice. It ignores the child and even rejects him or her in favor of some other version. This is painfully obvious when parents insist on perfection. "Every child should grow up feeling it's not a tragedy, not a catastrophe, to make a mistake," notes Dr. Maxwell R. Brand of New Jersey. "It's best to let a child drop a plate and then help clean it up. Better to have a broken plate than a broken child."

Mistakes are inevitable. They are also opportunities to learn. Self-confidence comes from dealing with mistakes constructively, not from never making a mistake. If you grew up in a home where mistakes were catastrophes, you no doubt see the consequences in yourself. As a parent, you can break that cycle with your children and in the process learn to relax with your own mistakes. "Parents, never drive your children to resentment but in bringing them up correct them and guide them as the Lord does" (Eph. 6:4, JB).

Children look to adults—teachers and particularly parents—to establish boundaries. Children become uncomfortable and anxious when they don't have limits. They don't know where to stand or where they stand. There is nothing wrong with saying no to a child, but it must be a reasonable and consistent *no*. Rather than rules for rules' sake, children have a right to rules that make sense and that promote personal safety, fulfillment, and family harmony.

A list of questions drawn up by the Easter Seal Society can help uncover flaws in family discipline. The questions may point up what happened in your own growing-up experience and can lead to corrections if you are a parent (or a teacher who deals with children). The appropriate answer to these questions is yes. If you can't answer affirmatively, give it some thought.

Do I set up reasonable rules for my child?

Do I speak in a firm, calm voice when I want my child to obey?

Do I tell the truth?

Do I ration my no's and allow reasonable behavior as often as I can?

Do father and mother have the same set of rules?

Am I consistent in punishment for repeated identical infractions?

Do I set realistic goals?

Do I set a good example myself?

Children grow up, and rules that once had to be obeyed on a parent's say-so must give way to understanding the why of rules. Infants obey blindly, but children grow in knowledge and should be encouraged to understand the reasons behind the rules. More and more, self-discipline replaces blind obedience, and to deprive a child of an internal gyroscope is to stunt his or her growth in maturity. A parent is preparing to let go; a child is preparing to be on his or her own, just as in that exciting moment when a parent stands back and a toddler takes the first steps. Learning to walk is really the parable for growing up.

But it is not easy to let go; a certain risk is involved on both sides. The child may fall. The parent may feel responsible and guilty. Probably the greatest challenge parents face is teaching their children to think and act for themselves. Dr. Bennett Olshaker describes the "greatest gift" adults can give children: " . . . the ability to stand on their own two feet so that they no longer need us."

Parents have the job of helping children reach the point where they can tackle the task of shaping tomorrow's world—if necessary as a "majority of one." Parents are sending out ambassadors, individuals who will spread the "good word" of love to the world. The values that children grow up to spread are not acquired in a vacuum. Faith and a longing to do something for others ordinarily show themselves in children because they were first present in the parents or in other adults who served as role models.

Religious values can't be faked. If parents have a lively sense of God, a constancy in prayer, a sound religious knowledge, and a keen instinct for justice, their children will reflect such influences. They will be far more likely to find in their faith a strength for meeting the pressures of life, and through the love of their parents they will have developed the capacity to love others as themselves.

Another dimension to this parent-child cycle has been added by the increase in life expectancy. At an age when men and women would have been dead and buried in the recent past, they are alive and well, and so are their parents. In 1900, the average American lived to age forty-seven; today the average is over seventy.

As a result, the child of yesterday can be the responsible adult of today in two ways—for his or her own children and for his or her own parents. Many adults who are grandparents themselves find one or more of their own parents still living. They are literally aging together with their own parents.

This experience means opportunities to begin or to restore close family relationships. Family members face the challenge of continuing to grow as individuals and also to grow closer to one another. Along the way, adult sons and daughters and their parents must cope with independence, finances, loneliness, living space, health, and aging. The following general guidelines can be helpful, but as in all close relationships, both generations must work together:

Be realistic. Asking too much is as undesirable as giving too little; asking too little is as undesirable as giving too much. The trick is to establish a balance between need and supply. Researchers have found that treating the elderly as helpless can be "psychologically devastating." Sometimes aging parents are treated as "children," which undermines them and puts grown sons and daughters into the position of being "parents" to their own mothers and fathers. The opposite also happens: aging parents may insist on continuing to treat adult sons and daughters as "children." A realistic assessment of a particular situation avoids both extremes.

Recognize that living is a process. Whether we are young or old, it is a mistake to think that the mood of the moment—our own or that of others—is permanent. Ups and downs, moments of darkness and of bright sunshine, unfold continually. Everyone can profit by moving beyond the hurt of the present and by preparing for better times. This includes willingness to forgive—whether or not you can forget—even deep-seated injuries.

Be ready for discovery. A fresh outlook can prevent being bored with each other or locked into a resentful or sullen attitude. Each encounter with a family member can be a "new ball game" if you let it. Don't take the other for granted; let something new happen.

Laugh a little. Humor makes a wonderful contribution to human relations. It puts things into perspective—painlessly. Such a realization can move you toward changing attitudes, actions, and reactions.

Be a friend. In friendship, each accepts the other as he or she is. Each can honestly communicate thoughts, feelings, needs, memories, and beliefs. A friend is ready to excuse, trust, hope, and endure. Friendship is a special something that family members can provide one another.

Put yourself in the other person's place. You feel differently at forty-five than you do at seventy-five. Different perspectives mean different viewpoints. As family members confront one another, it matters where they stand in their life histories. Differences can cause difficulty, but putting yourself in another's place can produce understanding. St. Francis of Assisi prayed, "Grant that I may not so much seek to be understood as to understand."

As past, present, and future weave in and out, the family's preserving and healing powers predominate. Society needs the family, and the individual needs the family. As the English journalist G. K. Chesterton commented, "The men and women who, for good reasons and bad, revolt against the family are, for good reasons and bad, simply revolting against mankind."

‹ 3 ›

The Time of Your Life

At some point in your life you realize, with a jolt, that your life is really yours to use in any way you choose. Family, friends, teachers, and mentors can all be helpful at various stages and in particular situations. They can provide the benefit of their experience, offer sound advice, warn about pitfalls, stand as role models. But they can't live your life for you.

Eventually, you must acknowledge the unsettling grandeur of the challenge: "It's my life."

You can't blindly follow the words and actions of others. You can't satisfy yourself by blaming the past or the hand life has dealt you. You can't blame someone else all the time. Such responses all lead to a dead end.

You can, instead, discover within yourself powers that you never realized existed. You can respond to perplexing problems in new and creative ways. You can rise to heights of achievement for yourself and for others. You can astonish others and yourself by realizing the potential inside you. Or you can mumble and grumble, find excuses, play the blaming game, give up.

The choice is yours to make. There is really no place to hide. Your life is yours to make or break. God will surely help you, but you enable the divine spirit to act within and through you. However indispensable is God's assistance, you yourself must carry through the actions that constitute a life fulfilled in meaningful action. "I can do all things in him who strengthens me" (Phil. 4:13, RSV).

In other words, you are free to squander or to use the gift of time. That precious commodity exists to be used in the present tense. You have no time but the present in which to grow and to help others grow. *Now* is "the time of your life."

"Most of us spend 58 minutes an hour living in the past with regret for lost joys, or shame for things badly done (both utterly useless and weakening) or in a future which we either long for or dread," notes the English novelist Margaret Storm Jameson. "The only way to live is to accept each minute as an unrepeatable miracle, which is exactly what it is—a miracle and unrepeatable."

In Ecclesiastes 3:1–8, the Bible acclaims a marvelous and meaningful approach to time. "There is a season for everything" —a time for giving birth, a time for dying; a time for planting, a time for uprooting; a time for tears, a time for laughter; a time for keeping, a time for throwing away; a time for being silent, a time for speaking.

That is the story of everyone's life, a universal drama that is shared in an individual way by everyone alive. Crucial events and major stages exist in every life. Some are inevitable and predictable—adolescence, leaving home, marriage, children, retirement, death. Others are unexpected—a major illness, the loss of a job, a broken relationship, a promotion, falling in love, a religious conversion. Today is the time to act and to live by responding.

A TIME TO CHOOSE

Each day offers opportunities to choose to live rather than to succumb to events. Repeatedly in small ways, sometimes in major personal ways, the choice is yours—to live or to exist. You can take charge of your life if you seek alternatives rather than take what happens for granted. You can only be responsible for yourself if you make choices and act on the choices.

A heart attack made Jess Lair, a thirty-five-year-old executive, choose to quit his job and begin a new career. While in the hospital, he reviewed his life and decided, "From now on I am never again going to do something that I don't deeply believe in." He and his family drastically cut back on their way of living so he could go to graduate school and earn a Ph.D. in psychology. Then they moved from Minneapolis to Montana where Jess landed a teaching job at the state university. For his students, Lair wrote the story of how his life was turned around: *I Ain't Much, Baby—But I'm All I've Got.* It obviously struck a responsive chord among many people, for the book became a best seller.

A TIME TO MAKE WAVES

At times, everyone feels uncertain, befuddled, even lost. Sister Dorothy Davis calls such restlessness and longing "God's signposts"—times of thrashing about in order to get your bearings, of making waves so that you can find the right direction.

A sailor makes waves when he is in a small boat surrounded by fog and is unable to see the buoys that mark his course. He turns his boat rapidly in small circles, knowing that the waves he makes will rock any buoy in the vicinity. Then he stops, listens, and repeats the procedure until he hears the buoy clang. In that way, he finds his direction.

Doing the same in life can lead to a sense of direction, thereby turning uncertainty into a search with a positive outcome. Circling a problem or a situation, talking to others, examining various possibilities, putting aside what was taken for granted—all can make waves in your life. They also are part of finding your way.

A TIME TO QUESTION

From time to time, crucial events will bring you up short. Or a chance remark may trigger questions about what you are doing with your life and where you are going. Here are some questions you can ask yourself about your *self:*

Do I tend to blame someone else for what's wrong in my life?

Do I try to change other people rather than my own attitudes and actions?

Am I willing to assume responsibility for the direction of my life?

Do I live in the present moment, or are most of my thoughts about either the past or the future?

Do I try to manipulate others into making my decisions for me so that I can blame them if things don't work out?

Do I confront the crises of life, or do I use alcohol, pills, sex, or other escapes?

Do I believe that whatever happens in my life—no matter how painful—I will be given the ability to cope?

A TIME TO BE OPEN

A French naturalist once conducted an experiment with insects called "processional caterpillars." He led them onto the rim of a large flowerpot in such a way that the leader was nose-to-tail with the last caterpillar in the procession. Through force of instinct they circled the rim for seven days and nights, without once breaking ranks to eat the visible supply of food nearby. As a result, they died of exhaustion and starvation.

People often justify the way something is done because "that's the way it's always been done." Or they do something because "that's what everyone else does." But there is a time to be open to alternatives, to see things afresh as if looking at them for the first time. Strive to earn the compliment that Paul Tillich paid his fellow theologian Karl Barth: "He refused to become his own follower."

A TIME TO CHANGE

"The process of growing up and growing older involves a series of changes," writes Dr. Frederic F. Flach in *The Secret Strength of Depression.* "Every transitional phase of life from childhood to marriage to old age requires some degree of giving up or letting go."

Trying to *hang on* when the time has come to *move on* can trip you up. Letting go can free you—and others—for the process of living fully. Probably the hardest thing to let go is an *if* feeling, wishing that your situation were different and wondering what your life would be like *if* you had more time, *if* you were younger (or older), *if* you were richer, luckier, smarter, and so on. Your real option begins by facing what is. Your course of action depends on what you have and what you can do. Your opportunities lie in being ready to risk change.

Change means uncertainty, since you can never be sure of the outcome, but change also opens up opportunities.

A TIME TO BELIEVE

Pollution, wars, racial and political conflict, economic ups and downs, crime rates, family breakdown—crises like these have people feeling that their world is "in trouble." Solutions must be sought within the self, in relationships with others, and with the loving Creator who sustains men and women in being. Renewed by contact with the realm of the spirit, you can bring more energy and insight to actions that must be taken.

Spend at least three minutes a day in prayerful reflection, more if you can. Focus on a quality you want to cultivate or a weakness you want to uproot. Reflect on a biblical quotation or a useful remark. (You may want to focus on some of the quotes in this book.) Start right away. You can immediately demonstrate that "the time is now."

Even resolutions that are not kept serve as guidelines and goals. The resolutions proposed in the eighteenth century by the noted American Puritan, Jonathan Edwards, still have a fresh ring:

> Resolved, to live with all my might while I do live.
> Resolved, never to do anything I should despise or think meanly of in another.
> Resolved, never to do anything out of revenge.
> Resolved, never to do anything which I should be afraid to do if it were the last hour of my life.

To underline how precious time is in your life, consider what happens to all the years by the time you are seventy. By then you will have spent nearly one quarter of a century sleeping—about twenty-three years for the average person—which leaves the following distribution of waking hours over a seventy-year period:

11 years working
8 years in recreation
6 years eating
5 1/2 years grooming
3 years being educated
3 years reading
3 years talking
1/2 year worshiping God

While any such estimate only gives a general impression of what actually happens in a lifetime, it emphasizes the universal fact that people spend their lives doing the same things. The above accounting covers sixty-three of the seventy years in just about everyone's life.

What's important is not *what* is done but *how* it is done. Those precious years can be well spent or misspent. It's your choice to make what you will of them, to take charge of your life and your time.

Even the amount of time spent sleeping is more under your

control than you would normally realize. As science writer Gay G. Luce has reported, not everyone needs eight hours of sleep a night. "Sleep quotas cannot be pinpointed by social custom," she notes. "Many people can function beautifully on three hours a night. Some need fourteen hours." Assuming that everyone needs the same amount of sleep is as unrealistic as buying a pair of shoes of "average size."

Maybe you need only a few hours' sleep, maybe more. When you're tired, rest. By all means get the amount of sleep you need, but when you get up, get going. A world in need of doers is no place for those who are groggy and yawn.

After time spent sleeping, you spend more of your life working than doing anything else. That makes work—in the house, on the job, in the office—a major part of your life. However, as a wise career counselor has pointed out, "The issue is not simply how you will make a living, it is also how you will make a life."

Whether your collar is blue or white, whether your efforts are in office work, housework, or homework, three basic qualities characterize a humanly fulfilling work situation. These were outlined by Dr. David Whitsett of Behavioral Science Technology, Inc.:

1. It is a complete piece of work. That is, it is a piece of work that has an identifiable beginning and end for the person doing the job. . . .

2. . . . it is one in which the worker has as much decision-making control over how he is to carry out the above defined piece of work as possible.

3. . . . it is one in which the individual receives frequent, direct feedback on his performance.

Work, by its nature, is not demeaning. Far from it, work is the means by which God enables you to take part in the ongoing task of creation, of "building the earth." But this does not deny the reality that *jobs* can be poorly designed and can lack purpose, freedom, or responsibility.

The other side of the coin is your attitude toward your job. A job is "only a job" until competence is harnessed to a driving desire to serve others. Then it is transformed by personal outlook and vision into a vocation. For example:

A railroad conductor wrote The Christophers that "you are so right in making known to people in all walks of life how important they are in the lives of others." In his job he is "dedicated to seeing that all passengers are comfortable and delivered safely to their destination with the courtesy that bespeaks human decency."

A children's book authority is campaigning for better children's literature. Her blood "runs cold" when she sees books that tend to "dehumanize the children" and leave them with "an impression that human beings are not important."

An office worker is trying to create an atmosphere of charity among associates: "There is so much 'hate' in our office. I sometimes come home sick. The petty bickering and the stabs in the back are getting intolerable for many of the people. But I'm not giving up hope for changing this."

A trade unionist is stirring up interest among members in running their own union.

A radio broadcaster writes of trying "to light one little candle in the darkness"—literally, since he conducts a midnight-to-5-A.M. program. He features "a blend of quality music—everything from the finer 'pops' to the classics."

A parking attendant makes a point of letting drivers know where to find vacant spaces in a multiramp garage. Said one woman driver: "Of all the fellows on this job, you're the only one that tells the customer where to find a spot, and I appreciate you're doing that."

There is no denying that many persons feel trapped in their jobs, leading what Thoreau called "lives of quiet desperation." One poll found job dissatisfaction among 40 percent of the workers surveyed; another places it at 16 percent. Certainly the signs of dissatisfaction show up in absenteeism, lateness, assembly-line sabotage, production snafus, alcoholism, and drug abuse. Union leaders are confronted by worker discontent, and management consultants cite lack of motivation among executives at various levels.

Sometimes you can change your attitude; sometimes you have to change jobs; sometimes you can change the circumstances at work. Whatever, it makes sense to assess your situation. Here are some well-seasoned suggestions:

1. *Take time to think.* Reflect on what you are doing; try to get a sense of where it fits in, what it means to others, and what difference it makes. There is hardly any work that does not in some way affect others. Try to see the connection between your work and others. An electric utility employee explained his job this way: "When you flip on the switch, I'm the guy who gives you the power." A bus driver on a commuter line said, "This city runs because I bring the guys who make the decisions in each morning and home every night." Thinking your situation over will help you get your bearings on how you really feel about your work and will help you identify what meaning it has for you.

2. *Ask some hard questions.* Is the job itself at fault? Is it your boss or is it you? Have you failed to extend yourself? If you were in your boss's shoes, what would be your attitude? What does the job have to offer? Are you doing it only for the money? When do you enjoy the job? What can you do to increase those times?

3. *Look around carefully.* Consider whether or not you are as "locked" into your job as you think. Many women have taken the lead in reexamining what it means to be a housewife and have opened up new horizons for themselves. Discontented job-holders may find they have to stay put—at least for the present—or they may discover alternatives, but this only comes from looking around carefully.

4. *Consider the risk.* The economist's favorite saying is worth pondering: There is no such thing as a free lunch. A price must be paid in one way or another when making changes. Greater

challenges mean greater risk, more work, and less security. Some people may actually prefer to stay put rather than take risks. That is up to them, but they should at least be honest with themselves, face their choice, and adjust to it.

5. *Check your options.* Starting where you are, search out opportunities. Transfers as well as promotions can change your job world without changing employers. Try harder. Suggest better methods of doing the job. Offer to take on additional responsibilities. Apply for openings in other departments or other parts of the company; see if you can redesign your own job. None of these are guaranteed to solve your particular situation, but unless you check for options, you will never find them.

6. *Prepare thoroughly.* Further education or special training may be needed before you switch jobs, especially if you change fields. Talking over the pros and cons with family and well-informed friends can help put the question into perspective. Meanwhile, you must meet the demands of your current job as you decide on a course of action. Any decision is in your hands, and you must be prepared to live with the consequences.

Of course, as important as work is, it is only part of the human story. Jesuit philosopher Walter J. Ong has noted that "work is what is not play and play is what is not work." Then he adds that even that contrast is too simple. The best players become professionals and *work* at their game. The best workers are those for whom work is a kind of *play*. Father Ong adds, "God's work is always play in the sense that it is always joyous, spontaneous, and completely free."

Play is an activity done for its own sake, for the sheer joy of doing it. It is a magnificently human and enriching side of life and a means by which you *re-create* your self. By engaging in activities that imitate life, the child learns about life; he or she imitates a parent, a teacher, a doctor, a bus driver. Adults also gain from play, from enjoying themselves. The challenge in our spectator society is to go beyond passive into active recreation. Play serves everyone well as a reminder of the joy in living. "For the joyous heart it is festival always" (Prov. 15:15, JB).

Not only in work and play do you face the challenge of taking command of your life. So too with eating, grooming, learning, reading, and talking. Each of these activities can be vital and meaningful. Each can be subverted by junk in food, reading matter, grooming products, topics of conversation, entertainment, and mass media.

Everyone participates in these basic areas of life. If everyone tried to follow the rule, "Thou shalt not deal in junk," then change would begin where it must—with the individual. The responsibility for upholding and raising the standards of society rests with you and me.

John W. Gardner, former Secretary of Health, Education, and Welfare, has observed: "The society which scorns excellence in plumbing because plumbing is a humble activity and tolerates shoddiness in philosophy because it is an exalted activity will have neither good plumbing nor good philosophy. Neither its pipes nor its theories will hold water."

You as a consumer and participant in the life around you can ask yourself the following questions:

Do I use a critical eye in what I eat, read, watch, and talk about?

Do I try to be informed? Do I try to keep up with knowledgeable opinion so that I can develop my critical faculties?

Do I support organizations that are trying to curb abuses and bring about reforms?

Do I try to maintain a balanced diet—not only in what I eat but in what I read, watch, and use?

Most important, am I taking charge of my life, assuming responsibility for it, paying attention to that responsibility, and doing something about it? Remember, *now* is "the time of your life."

⟨ 4 ⟩

Your Attitudes

Unless you have a positive, hopeful view of life and yourself, you are likely to feel that you can't cope. You can feel personally so beleaguered that you turn a rut into a deep hole and then dig in deeper instead of digging out.

Many people give up without really trying to take charge of situations and of their lives because they lack self-confidence. They are, in effect, denying their uniqueness, and specialness and are turning their backs on the time of their lives. Self-doubt is nothing less than a preparation—even a self-fulfilling prophecy —for disappointment and defeat. It also infects relationships with others, for without confidence in self you have nothing on which to base confidence in other people.

This self-inflicted handicap is so pronounced that psychologist Alexander Thomas has reported: "Lack of self-confidence is a nationwide problem. It is perhaps the most common psychological problem in America."

You've probably heard people express their lack of self-confidence in words like these:

"I never do anything right." Nothing at all? Sit back and think for a moment. Look back over your day, week, month, year. Have there been mistakes? Of course. A person who has never made

mistakes is a person who has never tried to do anything. The meaningful question isn't whether or not you made mistakes, but whether you learned from them. Then, what about the things you've done right? Start looking at them.

"I'm a failure." That's a matter of definition, mainly your own. The only real failure is to give up. Most children read biographies of famous people. The one persistent theme in these stories is that in the face of tremendous difficulties these people refused to give up. That's why they succeeded and why their lives are worth reading about. What's crucial is to keep pursuing a goal once you know what it is.

"I'll only make matters worse." That's an easy excuse for not acting. It's a self-defeating habit of putting yourself down. It's a backward-looking view of life that usually guarantees its own accuracy. It becomes an expectation that shapes actions or inactions and decides—in advance—how you'll feel about any outcome.

You and I often spend more time giving excuses or finding reasons why a job can't be done than in sitting down seriously and trying to figure out how to do the job. Sometimes this kind of outlook goes by the name of *worry*. Worry keeps you from acting. Sometimes it's justified; many times it's not.

Dr. Thomas S. Kepler did a study about people's worries, and he found out the following:

Forty percent of your worries will never happen. Thirty percent concern people's criticism of you. Twelve percent are over decisions that you've already made. Ten percent are about your health.

That accounts for 92 percent of all worries, and little or nothing can be done about them. The other 8 percent are worth thinking about and acting on. That eliminates over 90 percent of the feelings that keep you from being your best possible self. Alcoholics Anonymous uses the following prayer, composed by Reinhold Niebuhr in 1934. It has helped many people who had allowed worry to drive them to drink:

O God, give us serenity to accept what cannot be changed, courage to change what should be changed, and wisdom to distinguish the one from the other.

Overcoming anxieties and building self-confidence are lifelong tasks, but the process can begin immediately, here and now. The following five-step program was devised by a management expert:

1. Make an inventory of your accomplishments as well as your assets as an individual. This provides a positive and realistic starting point—and it will also make you feel better.

2. Single out one personal deficiency or weakness and concentrate on removing that or improving yourself in that particular area.

3. Increase your knowledge of the area you're involved in or the one that gives you the most concern. Lack of information can prevent you from tackling something new or from applying skills and talents you already have.

4. Take on an assignment you once considered too difficult. This will be a good test of how well you've progressed on the first three steps.

5. Pay some attention to your personal appearance: the way you dress, the way you walk, even the way you talk. This all reflects on the way you feel about yourself. If you look better and sound better, it probably means you'll feel better about yourself —and other people will too.

There are no magic remedies that will enable you to build self-confidence, self-esteem, and the right kind of self-love. They must have fertile soil in which to blossom, and they must have the nourishment of faith in yourself, in other people, and in God. They must come from within; nobody can give them to you. With God's help you can harness your vast potential for good.

An elderly preacher knew this secret, and each day he used to get up and say this prayer: "Lord, help me to remember that nothing is going to happen today that you and I together can't handle."

A positive self-image is essential if you are really going to act to change yourself and the world around you. Much of self-image is a matter of personal perspective. Once when Oliver Wendell Holmes was attending a meeting in which he was the shortest man present, a friend quipped, "Dr. Holmes, I should think you'd feel rather small among us big fellows." Looking around at the group, Holmes responded, "I do. I feel like a dime among a lot of pennies."

Like Dr. Holmes, you have your own particular set of physical, mental, and spiritual characteristics. You have both assets and liabilities. Thank God for your assets and ask for his help in overcoming the liabilities. You can get much more done for many more people if you spend more time doing what can be done and less time being concerned about what can't be done. Moreover, what could be called liabilities may well be assets. As Holmes did, you can discover and identify the positive side of your characteristics rather than dwell on the negative.

One man, in writing to The Christophers, told how fearful he was when he went to his first political meeting. "My heart pounded, my knees knocked, and my voice trembled," he wrote. But instead of sitting there with his worries, he decided that he had a point of view he wanted to express to the group. With a shaky voice, he got up and started talking. This is what he found out: "Everytime I got up to speak, it got easier, and gradually, as people listened, I began to gain confidence. Eventually I found I had the ability to speak out when I thought something wasn't right."

That's the kind of attitude and action our world needs. Wanted: people with positive ideas and attitudes to take a constructive part in political, educational, and religious life, in decision making on every level—local, state, national, even global.

There are too many problems in the world for you to allow yourself the luxury of a false humility that will keep you from making the contributions that other people have a right to expect of you. Select something you consider difficult, and instead of worrying about what will happen, try it.

In building self-confidence, perseverance is needed. This is what the celebrated Spanish violinist Pablo de Sarasate meant when he answered a famous critic who called him a genius. "Genius," he snorted. "For thirty-seven years I've practiced fourteen hours a day, and now they call me a genius." No matter how many gifts you have and no matter how much you want to make up for your shortcomings, you're not going to get far unless you persevere.

It's only sensible to recognize that you can't do *every*thing; yet with the proper kind of self-confidence, you realize that you can do *some*thing. If you are willing to persevere day after day and year after year, you learn that unremitting practice can achieve many different goals.

Consider the example of Judy Miller of Bowling Green, Ohio, who experienced a profound change in her consciousness. Although she recognized that her talents were not particularly outstanding, she began to realize that she did in fact possess talent—"a quiet, precious gift of being able to do many small things well. I began to appreciate being me. Me was O.K. Ordinary can be beautiful too. I am a fine unique person, who just never truly appreciated the beauty of her own individuality."

As Judy Miller became comfortable with herself; she could be comfortable with others. She was ready—as you can be ready —to reach out to others in a direct, honest way, to find in them the positive aspects she had discovered in herself. She was in a position, not only to be confident, but to begin building the confidence and strength of others.

Her path is instructive. "When did it happen," she asks, "that slow realization that not all of us *have* to possess earth-shaking talent? That without talent, as I had always defined it, we were still worthwhile human beings?"

She began to notice important small things. Her daughter

saying, "You're the best mom ever." Her best friend saying, "What would I do without you to talk with?" Someone else commenting on the fine job she was doing in raising her daughter. Slowly, over the years, she began to notice—her success as a mother, her pleasure in planting and tending a garden, in long country walks, in the company of her friends. She realized she was "happy." She "began to understand how wonderful it was to have the respect and esteem of close friends" and to enjoy the skill she did have.

What happened to Judy Miller can happen to anyone who accepts who she or he is and views her or his abilities in a positive light. The next stage inevitably follows. In the spillover, one wants others to feel the same. One wants to help others develop self-confidence. Feeling good about yourself means you don't feel threatened by others. You recognize and respond to the positive aspects in them.

There are many opportunities to build up rather than tear down. Parents can find good things to say about each of their children and encourage them to develop their talents. Teachers can find that little spark of creativity in a student and encourage him or her to use it. (Comedian Steve Allen once recalled with a glow a seventh-grade parochial school teacher in Chicago who saw some of Steve's poetry and told him he had a great talent and to be sure to develop it. And he did.) An employer who discovers in an employee an ability that does not fit his or her particular job can transfer that individual to a situation where the ability can be used.

Building up other people means neither flattery nor insincerity. It has nothing to do with "buttering up people," which everyone naturally shrinks from because it's insincere and phony. It's another matter to honestly encourage the talents and attractive traits you find in others.

Calling forth the latent talents of others is not the same thing as indiscriminate applause that says one is the best child, the best person, the best whatever in the entire world. What means something is specific and thoughtful praise: "I like you because you really listen when I talk, and that makes me feel good." Everyone needs honest affirmation that is not only complimentary but that expresses some appreciation of the spark God has put in every human being. Praise nourishes the good quality. Mark Twain once said that he could live for three months on a compliment.

A famous example of the power of a compliment concerns Edward Steichen who eventually won great renown as a photographer. On the day he shot his first pictures, only one out of fifty could be considered halfway decent. His father suggested that Edward put away the camera and try another hobby. But his mother was impressed by one photograph of his sister at the piano and said that it more than made up for the forty-nine others. Steichen's mother had the vision to spot the spark of excellence in the midst of failure and cared enough to point out a small achievement instead of dwelling on obvious shortcomings. Instead of a thoughtless put-down, she offered a gentle word of encouragement that led him to stay with his camera and eventually to become one of the world's greatest photographers.

With proper appreciation of yourself, you develop awareness that it is within your power to relate to others in a warm, loving manner. You realize that the larger world of neighborhood and school, of politics and economics, of town, nation, and global community all have some claim on your concern and your constructive influence and action.

⊰ 5 ⊱

Deciding to Show the Way

Orville Kelly lived with his wife and four children in Burlington, Iowa. A forty-three-year-old newspaper editor involved in his family, in his work, in his community, in life itself until a medical diagnosis shattered his world. The doctor told him he had an incurable cancer of the lymph system. This death notice drove Orville into black depression and emotional paralysis until he decided to "stop thinking about dying and start thinking about life."

After he published a story in his local newspaper suggesting that people with "incurable" diseases should have an organization in which they could help each other, his idea received national attention. He became founder of Make Today Count (MTC), which grew to three thousand five hundred members in seventy chapters all over the country. Cancer patients, their families, clergymen, and nurses belong to MTC, meeting once or twice a month to discuss how to confront "life-threatening illness."

In deciding to show the way, Orville Kelly became influential in the fullest sense of the word. He became a leader by serving and by exemplifying his message of making each day count. He began writing and making speeches to keep up with the letters, phone calls, and invitations that came from all over the country.

"Maybe when ordinary people see me, they see an ordinary guy who has made ordinary mistakes in life," he said, "and they say if I can do it [face death], then maybe they can do the same thing." When MTC members meet, they "drink coffee and laugh a lot," he reported. "We may talk about each other's illness, but we might talk about going hunting too. The idea is just to be normal."

The kind of leadership dramatized by Orville Kelly is found in infinite shapes and forms. A retired New Jersey tailor wrote a textbook on his trade to help the hard-core unemployed find "security and a future." An Ohio woman successfully headed a drive to convert an unused railroad station into a library. A San Diego mother started a club for girls who had nowhere to go. A hot-dog vendor in East Harlem provided twenty dollars a month to keep a neighborhood study club open. A successful artist decided to enrich the lives of older persons by teaching them how to paint. A legal aid attorney recruited lawyers for night duty to help those who work all day and can only see a lawyer at night. A sixty-year-old Englishwoman decided to do something about a massive traffic jam in front of her home when the police did not respond: "I just waved my arms about and things began to move. Some of the lines were a mile long, and the motorists who had been waiting ages thanked me as they passed."

It is not easy to define leadership, but we all recognize a leader. Leadership arises when an individual works with others to take the right action at the right moment to meet some human need. Effective leadership tends to multiply itself rather than to keep power carefully hoarded. Leadership gives people a positive vision about the world or a problem and points the way to making improvements. Leadership also helps provide people with the tools and means by which they can start to work out solutions to problems. Positive leadership praises those who have in fact done a good job, especially when they do it even better than a leader.

Leaders are not born; they're made. It is more accurate to say that they make them*selves*. Each person, you in your own way, with God's help, in your own particular circumstances in life, can in some real way become a leader. You do it by using what you have, by finding ways in which you can fulfill your potential, by bringing out the best in others. "Having gifts that differ according to the grace given us, let us use them" (Rom. 12:6, RSV).

Leaders confront the realities of life around them.

The *problem* is not only "out there" but "right here," not only with "them," but with "you," "me," "us." As Pogo said in the comic strip, "I have seen the enemy, and it is us."

The vitality and the progress of any community and of any society results from the vision and the active commitment of countless persons in all walks of life. Many are called, and many are needed.

Pinpointing abuses is only the beginning, not the solution. Persistent, constructive efforts are necessary.

From the highest to the humblest office, from the extraordinary to the everyday, the moral strength of a people demands that the selfish attitude be replaced by the selfless act. "Ask not what your country can do for you; ask what you can do for your country," President John F. Kennedy told America at his inauguration.

A society is best served by leaders who do just that—serve —rather than act out of vainglorious or self-seeking motives.

The highest forms of leadership—at any level—draw out the finest qualities, both human and spiritual, of others.

In Mark 10:42-45: "You know that those who are supposed to rule over the Gentiles lord it over them, and their great men exercise authority over them. But it shall not be so among you; but whoever would be great among you must be your servant, and whoever would be first among you would be the slave of all. For the Son of man also came not to be served but to serve, and to give his life as a ransom for many" (RSV).

While leadership begins in awareness of a need and in the motivation "to do something about it," the road to effective leadership is paved with more than good intentions. You must grasp the dynamics of leadership and develop the skills of putting across your messages.

To assess leadership capabilities and to work toward them, here are some questions to ask yourself. If you give a favorable answer to all of them, you're probably being unrealistic. Don't be discouraged if you find you don't live up to all of them as much as you would like. The important thing is to stop and think, to try to answer these questions honestly, and to seek ways in which you can answer them more favorably at the same time next year.

Are you open to alternative actions, opportunities, and solutions? Or do you tend to go on doing the same thing without evaluating and reevaluating what you are doing?

Do you welcome the ideas of others and listen to what sound like wild suggestions?

Can you sense the roots of other people's uneasiness and define the basic problem?

Can you give credit where credit is due for useful ideas and effective labors?

Are you willing and able to delegate authority and to give others both the freedom and the means to accomplish a goal?

Do you encourage the faint-hearted while diplomatically restraining the overenthusiastic?

Do you try to reconcile clashing viewpoints rather than take sides or become a special pleader?

Can you summarize trends and clearly mark out points of essential difference?

Do you work out and accept realistic compromise without sacrificing moral principle?

Do you emphasize that each person has a contribution to make to the common effort?

Can you initiate change by starting with the familiar before moving into the unknown?

Do you inspire follow-through in those with whom you work?

Can you be trusted to keep a confidence?

Are you candid but cordial in limiting unjust criticism?

Do you try to bring out the best in people so that solutions may be found that serve God and honor humankind?

No matter where you are—at home, on the job, at school, in an organization, driving on an expressway or flying through the air—you can put your leadership potential to work. The more committed you are to serve others, the more alert you will be to leadership opportunities, the more imaginative you will be in discovering them. Take a second look at your neighborhood, community, school, organization, factory, office, and identify needs that can be met all around you.

You can find opportunities for serving by showing the way wherever you are. You could notice, as Lee Mendel did, that many older people in West Palm Beach, Florida, were forced to buy as their main meal the dog food he manufactured. They could not afford decent, nourishing food. So Mr. Mendel started a nonprofit cooperative to sell protein-rich sea food at economical prices. A sales force of elderly men was organized to work in a senior citizens cooperative, which also provided menus and recipes along with the sea food. For needy senior citizens, Lee Mendel made a difference.

Or you could be like Annie Mae Bankhead of College Station, Arkansas, who had to work in a factory and at domestic jobs to support her four children. But she still was able to do the following over a thirty-five-year period: bring her neglected town electricity, telephones, paved roads, and a water supply; help to set up a Head Start program; establish a community self-help organization; get a fire department and equipment; launch a voter education project; and transform a poor, backward all-black community into a growing integrated town. If anyone in College Station felt something had to be done, there was a standard answer: "Let's tell Bankhead." She had a profoundly simple motivation that was summed up in what her father used to tell her: "Make everywhere you live a better place."

To get started right where you are, follow the lead of the bumblebee, which doesn't realize that according to the applied laws of aerodynamics it should not be able to fly. According to its size, weight, and shape in relation to its total wingspread, this husky insect should not be able to get off the ground. The experts confirm this in laboratory tests; yet out in the real world, the bumblebee zooms through the air.

Don't underestimate yourself. If you must go to an extreme, go in the opposite direction: overestimate yourself. It's much easier to restrain enthusiasm than to create it. Since it began in 1945, the Christopher idea has been based on the lives of people who recognized a problem they could do something about and who were able to estimate properly their own importance. They tried, frequently failed, yet somehow succeeded in bringing about some beneficial difference in their neighborhood, city, or country. The story of The Christophers is the account of individuals who had enough confidence in God and in themselves to try to change at least part of the world for the better.

There are probably as many ways to put leadership into action as there are people who want to do it; so don't consider the following strategy as a formula set in concrete. It's only a start. You, with your experience and imagination, may come up with something better suited to you. Nonetheless, the following approach has proved useful:

Set a definite goal. After assessing yourself, your values, your attitudes, and the needs around you, identify a specific goal. It is only a start to set your sights on being the best you can be—parent, employee, business person, teacher, doctor, mechanic, sales person, whatever. Translate that goal into definite actions. It's not enough to aim at being the best possible parent; decide on particular things you will do (or not do) with your children.

It's not enough to aim at creating a positive atmosphere at work; identify what you can do when you arrive in the morning, which individuals you can help, what tasks you can undertake. Don't pave the road ahead with good intentions alone; go down that road with specific goal-directed steps.

Do your homework. The first responsibility of a leader is to get the facts. To call for others to follow you is to take on the duty of knowing what you are doing and why. To urge others to follow by using sound information and solid arguments is to earn the right to be heard—and followed. What author Leroy Ramsey said applies to leading as well as pleading: "Speaking with passion but without the facts is like making a beautiful dive into an empty pool."

Be realistic. Leadership calls for hard work, not for remote-control activity. The advertising slogan, "We Try Harder," put across its message by striking a responsive chord among large numbers of car renters. It is a basic American story that is summed up in comedian Sam Levenson's remark about his immigrant father who "came over here from the old country" and "found out three things: (1) that the streets were not paved with gold, (2) that most of the streets were not even paved, (3) that he had to help pave them."

Weigh the consequences. Actions produce reactions, accomplishments breed results, outcomes lead to aftermaths. Since leaders do not reach goals or work toward them without involving others, their responsibility is to consider the consequences of what they are doing. Look carefully. Make certain others will be able to follow and that others will not be hurt or victimized.

Be positive and constructive. The spirit of effective leadership is filled with love of people, faith in a better world, and hope of success. This means treating others with respect and with regard for their attitudes and viewpoints. Leaders reveal their attitudes toward others in their overall approach, in small gestures, and in critical moments.

Stick to priorities. Unless you are able to put first things first, your leadership will get bogged down in trivialities and distractions. Keeping your eye on the goal, you should judge issues and make decisions in terms of what you want to accomplish. Pray for the wisdom to know what to leave out. "I would have you wise as to what is good" (Rom. 16:19, RSV).

See things through. Preparation, analysis, planning, and an opening flourish only mean something when you continue down the road with your efforts. Worthwhile leaders see things through; when the going gets tough, the tough get going and try even harder.

All that has just been said should not be interpreted as a pat formula for success. Each person has to ask: What do I have to offer? What are my needs? What opportunities are open to me? Am I ready to overcome discouragement? You may find that the harder you try to provide a service for some people, the less they will pay attention. You may not get much thanks. You can almost be positive that you won't make headlines, and you can be certain that you won't make any more money. But once in a while somebody will find some small and meaningful way to say thanks, and that will be worth all the effort.

The test of this kind of leadership really comes down to the question of what is important in your life. You cannot live according to the expectations of others. Sooner or later you have to answer the double-barreled question: What do I want to do and how do I want to do it?

This kind of leadership begins within and moves out for its own sake, not for acclaim. Being *fulfilled* in leadership is not the same as being praised and publicized as a leader.

Probably no one has summed up this kind of leadership as well as Lao Tzu, the great Chinese philosopher of twenty-five hundred years ago who said:

> A leader is best
> When people barely know that he exists,
> Not so good

when people obey and acclaim him,
Worst when they despise him.
'Fail to honor people,
They fail to honor you;'
But of a good leader,
who talks little,
When his work is done,
his aim fulfilled,
They will all say,
"We did it ourselves."*

*From *The Way of Life: According to Lao Tzu*, trans. Witter Bynner (New York: The John Day Co., 1962), pp. 34–35. Reprinted by permission of T.Y. Crowell, Co., Inc.

‹ 6 ›

Getting Your Message Across

Each of us is a message center, receiving and sending continuously, just as regularly as breathing in and breathing out. By sight, sound, smell, touch, and taste, the traffic in communications is unceasing. It is a universal act of sharing, of exchanging facts, feelings, ideas, attitudes, reactions, and intentions, of exchanging the manifold aspects of humanity.

Communication, rooted in the Latin word *communis* meaning "common," is a proclamation of connectedness among all humans. It involves sender, message, medium, and receiver. While there is no stopping the process of human communication, there is no guarantee that messages arrive as intended. That is the never-ending challenge in communications: getting your message across.

No matter how worthy your intentions or wonderful your messages, in the final analysis your communications depend on what happens on the receiving end.

In a media-filled world, messages are often misunderstood, misdirected, mutilated. Instead of clear dispatches, *static* often fills the air, and noise or garbled reports are transmitted.

The word *static* tells the story. The opposite of static is *dynamic*. When there's static between two people, nothing moves; they are both rigid. In real communication, something dynamic happens; a part of one person flows to another, is absorbed, and flows back. Movement overcomes static. Suddenly there is a third thing to share that is greater than what either had to begin with.

You can do your share in clearing the air of static by making your messages clear, positive, and constructive. Reflect on what is involved in communications and broaden your understanding. Don't confine your definition to words, but extend it to *any behavior* that carries a message.

It has been estimated that when humans communicate 80 percent of the meaning is carried by nonverbal means (body language, tone of voice, facial expression). Sigmund Freud once said: "He that has eyes to see and ears to hear may convince himself that no mortal can keep a secret. If his lips are silent, he chatters with his finger tips; betrayal oozes out of him at every pore."

In his book *Family Communication,* Dr. Sven Wahlroos, a prominent psychologist, describes communication as "perhaps the most important of all topics in psychology." He adds: "It is largely through communication that we become what we are; it is through communication that we learn what we know; it is largely through destructive communication that problems in human relations are created, and it is through constructive communication that such problems are prevented or solved."

Dr. Wahlroos has set forth some communication rules that apply to all relationships, not just to those in the family.

Actions speak louder than words. Those around you know you best by your actions. To practice what you preach is to deliver the best sermon of all; not to practice what you preach is to deliver a boomeranging sermon. Think of the times you tune someone out because you don't believe they really mean what they are saying. To really mean what you say is to act on words, and to do that is to really get your message across.

Recognize that each event can be seen from different points of view. This is related to the old saw about two neighbors who never could agree on anything because they were arguing from different *premises.* By keeping an eye out for the other person's viewpoint, you can see your own in a more revealing light and get the benefit of a fresh look at the situation. This can prevent you from coming up against a stone wall when communicating. In effect, you can avoid speaking a different language when dealing with someone.

Accept all feelings and try to understand them; do not accept all actions, but try to understand them. In communicating, feelings play a dominant part, and the communicator who ignores feelings is going to be ignored. While you stand up and are counted on the basis of your principles and while you do not condone all actions on the part of others, you do want to create two-way traffic between you and others.

Make the effort to really listen. It is hard work, but it's necessary if communication is going to flow. Heed the warning of Northwestern University professor Bergen Evans: "We are all lying in wait to pick up the thread of our discourse that the other person so rudely interrupted." Unless you really enter the world of the other person and listen to what he or she is saying, unless you observe the other's reaction to your message, chances are you will talk only to yourself. We should strive to listen to others the way we want God to listen to us —with full attention.

Of course, some people are natural communicators. They seem to know at an early age how to get across to other people. But most of us learn by trial and error. When we try to get through to people with words and find that we are misunderstood, we try different ways to get our message across if we are really serious about the effort. And we pay even closer attention to our listeners. Gradually we can find out through long, hard, difficult attempts that while communicating is not easy it is possible.

As with any activity, skills take the mystery out of communicating. Communication begins with *thinking*—the skill that comes before the challenges of *speaking* and *writing*. When Ralph Waldo Emerson was asked what was the hardest thing in the world to do, his response was very simple: "To think." Basic to any communication is the quiet, sometimes lonely effort to analyze the facts and to understand your position. The mind should be set in gear before the mouth is put in motion.

A thinking person is guided by facts, no matter how unpalatable they may be. A thinking person realizes that the right way and the expedient way are not always the same. A thinking person learns from his or her mistakes and from the mistakes of others. A thinking person seeks feedback and is alert to the reactions of others in searching for and working toward solutions. A thinking person knows when to speak and when to keep silent, when to act and when to wait. A thinking person is humble enough to acknowledge wisdom in others and wise enough to realize that reality is greater than the sum total of his or her own knowledge and experience.

You must, of course, think for yourself, a strenuous and demanding process made exciting by the prospect of reaching a new understanding, a new awareness, a new solution.

To sharpen your skills in thinking, keep in mind the following guidelines:

1. Be honest with yourself. Avoid self-delusion.

2. Confront problems, don't evade them. Growth comes through facing reality.

3. Widen your interests. Stretch your mind by reading, talking with others, listening.

4. Write out the problem. Positive action depends on clear thinking. Spelling it out on paper helps.

5. Keep first things first. Concentrate on the main issues; don't be diverted by secondary matters or nonessentials.

6. Don't oversimplify. If a problem is serious enough to demand your attention, it's important enough to ponder in all its dimensions.

7. Get beyond faultfinding. People know what's wrong. They want to know what to do about it.

8. Keep an open mind. The best solution may not be *your* solution.

9. Retain your sense of humor. Humor can reduce prejudice, open channels of communication, put things in perspective.

10. Develop insight. Listen for what the other person means, not merely what he or she says.

11. Accentuate the positive. Emphasize points of agreement without ignoring significant differences.

12. Pray for solutions. God is the creator and source of all good things, right desires, and just works.

In a celebrated essay "Politics and the English Language," George Orwell warned of the vicious circle in which "foolish thoughts" produce "slovenliness" of language which in turn "makes it easier for us to have foolish thoughts." Thus, "if thought corrupts language, language can also corrupt." Since it works both ways, we must meet the challenge of clear language—written and spoken—as well as the challenge of clear thinking.

This task is not the exclusive concern of professional writers and speakers. Everyone must communicate in order to function in society. Anyone wanting to communicate ideas and to lead others must get messages across clearly and effectively.

The secret of communicating is that there is no secret—just planning, preparation, and practice. That is no easy matter, but it is not beyond anyone who makes the effort, podium jitters and writer's cramp notwithstanding. The best advice for learning how to speak and write is: *Do it.* But how? Here are some basic ground rules.

KNOW WHAT YOU WANT TO SAY

The hardest sentence to write is the first one; next in difficulty is the one that sums up what you want to say. Whether composing a speech or an article or a letter to the editor, pinpoint the theme of your message by writing it down in two or three sentences. Don't get bogged down on literary excellence; concentrate on accuracy and clarity. Even begin your summary with "I want to say . . ." or "My point is that. . . ." You may have to rewrite the summary several times to satisfy yourself. Each rewrite makes it clearer, uncovers shortcomings, increases your familiarity with the message. Out of familiarity comes greater confidence that helps to carry you through the writing or speaking process.

ORGANIZE YOUR MATERIAL

Identify the main points that develop your theme, and make a list of them. Decide on the order in which you will use them; sort out your material accordingly. Jacques Barzun, who has written so well about writing, has a worthwhile suggestion on outlines: don't make an all-inclusive master plan down to subheads and sub-subheads. Set down the main points only, with each point of equal weight and importance. For instance, the outline for this chapter boiled down to these main headings: explain communications; general communications rules; thinking; steps to follow; speaking; writing. These emerged from thinking through to a theme and arranging the main points in a logical order.

KEEP YOUR AUDIENCE IN MIND

Whether written or spoken, a message has the clearest flight when aimed carefully at your audience. Learn all you can about your audience: what their interests are, how much they know about the subject, how they stand on an issue, what their needs are, what they want to know. Talk *to* them rather than *at* them. If the audience is going to read your message, try to find out what approaches have succeeded best with them. Usually, a written message that will be published goes through a "gatekeeper"— someone who makes the decision to publish it. On a newspaper or magazine, it would be the editor; in an organization, it would be the president or some other administrative official. The "gatekeeper" is supposed to know the audience, and he or she has the power to close the gate on you. So find out what your "gatekeeper" wants, and remember the demand that all audiences make: Don't waste our time.

EXPRESS YOUR MESSAGE CLEARLY

You can write or say that "Simians indigenous to Zamboanga are destitute of caudal appendages" or that "Monkeys in Zamboanga have no tails." The example is exaggerated, but the danger of violating the iron rule of simplicity is real. Never use two words where one word will do the job, and always make that one word as simple as possible. Let the message make the wording complicated; don't let the wording make the message complicated. Focus on getting that message across; different messages dictate different presentation levels. Always remember the lesson of the greatest messages ever sent—those in the Bible. Profound truths about God and man and eternal verities are presented in the simplest language. Of course, meet the demands of grammar, the requirements of spelling and pronunciation, and the discipline of proper sentence and paragraph structure.

While no single formula should be followed blindly, there are standard ways to present a speech and to write a letter (as typical of all writing efforts). Each approach illustrates the way you can build clarity into your messages to make them effective.

In presenting a speech:

Capture attention. Your opening can create a receptive atmosphere or do the opposite. A striking statement, an arresting quote, or a winning story (the typical opening) can launch your speech.

Make your point. Sum up your talk in no more than three sentences, better still, one sentence that is repeated and rephrased for emphasis. Your audience then has no doubts about where you are going. As the lecturer's old saw puts it: Tell 'em what you are going to tell them; tell 'em; then tell 'em what you told them.

Build your case. In developing your main points, use both evidence and illustrations and be sure to add your own experiences wherever possible. This adds a note of conviction and a stamp of authenticity.

Keep it short. Use vivid words, easy-to-understand language, and "word pictures," but most of all, do not drag on. Make each point as forcefully and briefly as possible.

Dramatize. Use picture slides, films, photos, or tapes to underline your points (but be sure the audio-visual setup works smoothly).

Know when to stop. Be alert to audience reactions, and be sure to stop in time. No iron-clad time limit can be suggested for all talks; it depends on the subject, the audience, the occasion, and the content. But always err on the side of brevity.

Summarize. Repeat your main points in closing, and signal the audience that you are ending by reaching a climactic pitch. If, as a leader, you are urging action, end with your appeal and then specifically announce the ending. Some speakers add "Thank you" to avoid any doubts.

In writing a letter (or a memo or an article):

Introduce the topic. Let the reader know what the communication is all about from the start. A letter to a stranger should identify you and your connection with the topic. All written messages should immediately state their purpose.

Announce the theme. A summary paragraph should tell it all in capsule form.

Develop your theme. Present your main points in order, section by section. Don't let one section get out of hand. Try to weave in facts, figures, quotations, and anecdotes, depending on how long your written message is. Revise as often as necessary, for good writing is a matter of rewriting.

Conclude. Your main points should reach a conclusion, which can then lead to recommendations. Try to end emphatically with a quotation or a statement that reaffirms your theme, carrying it the extra step forward to the concluding note.

If you are serious about mastering written and spoken communication, you must be prepared to practice and to actually go ahead and deliver a speech or write something. The best advice is to start by doing and after each effort analyze what you have done. Get feedback from others. Try and try again. If you believe in what you are doing, if you are committed, if you want to make a contribution, then you will rise to the challenge of communicating.

As you get better in communicating, you will worry less and less about rules like the ones discussed in this chapter. You simply make them part of yourself; you use them automatically. You become sensitive to other people and attentive to precision in language and to clarity. You are loving toward the people with whom you are trying to share some idea, some feeling. You make an honest effort that reflects hard work and sensitivity. People sense such an effort and respond to it.

In sum, try to communicate as you would be communicated with. This is just another way of restating the Golden Rule.

⟨ 7 ⟩

Deciding on Your
Biggest Role—*You*

On the stage, actors are given lines to memorize, parts to play, directions to follow. They deliver the lines and perform the actions, but they do not write their roles. The roles have been devised by the playwright and interpreted by the director.

Real life is different, and the part you play is far more exciting than any stage production. You are playing yourself; no script dictates your actions, no one directs your performance. You write your role as you go along by the decisions you make.

In this way you express who you are and what you stand for. It is an exciting test that demands strength, devotion, and overall consistency. Instead of curtain calls, rounds of applause, and press notices, you will feel inside the reward for a performance that meets high standards. A full life, peace of mind, and a sense of fulfillment take the place of public acclaim.

Your role in life calls for choices, for deciding which positions to affirm, which way to turn, which actions to take. Those decisions come in many varieties, from the everyday to the soul-shattering, from those that flit across the brain so quickly that they are not noticed to those that involve personal agony.

Routine decisions are made easily, often without being noticed. According to the Colorado highway patrol, in the course of covering only one mile of highway, a driver makes twenty decisions. To begin the day, you pick a shirt and tie, decide on a dress or pantsuit, select a breakfast cereal, tune to a TV station. Such decisions never stop all day long.

Important decisions touch your ambitions, your hopes, your dreams, your entire way of life. Should you change jobs? Do you want to marry X? What position will you take on a controversial issue? Should you move to another city?

Making decisions means choosing. Each time you pick one road instead of another you point yourself and those close to you in a particular direction. The other roads have been excluded, the die cast. Rather than live with "might have beens" or "if onlys," try to make the best decisions you can and then live with them, confident that you have done your best.

Through the decisions you make, you achieve your identity, shape your autobiography, create your selfhood. You become an active participant in life and in God's universe. You help to make the world you live in as you either fulfill or move counter to God's plan.

Because decisions are a basic part of living, they are the stuff of both fiction and real life, the drumbeat of heroic action and the rhythm of biographies. The history of the United States is, in fact, the result of forty million decisions on the part of immigrants to uproot and come to America. Their choice changed them and changed America.

To take any mystery out of decision making, step back and reflect on what goes into a good decision. What is involved in a major choice is your entire self, your values, your personality, your self-esteem, and your sense of hope. You should try to involve the best of yourself in making a decision, and you should, in particular, not deny either facts or feelings.

All logic and no feeling can make for a hollow decision.

All feeling and no logic or facts can make for a foolish decision.

Reliable facts, adequate information, and a logical approach place a decision in a realistic context and cut down the chances for an unwise choice. Feelings and emotions can run roughshod over facts and logic, putting you in the position of the misguided wit who admits: "Don't confuse me with facts, my mind's already made up." Yet there is no denying the place of feelings which give personal meaning to decisions and which get you moving in carrying out a decision.

Imagination and flexibility—the ability to see new alternatives and to recognize ways in which they can be applied—help you over obstacles and help you to escape mental and emotional blocks. Dr. Edward de Bono, an authority on problem solving, describes the value of "lateral thinking," the ability to spot alternatives. With "vertical thinking," you continue to dig the same hole deeper. In "lateral thinking," you dig different holes in different places. Here are some de Bono questions to overcome mental blocks:

Is there any other way to express the problem?

What random ideas arise when you relax and let your mind wander around the problem?

Can you turn the problem upside down? Reverse it?

Can you shift the emphasis from one part of the problem to another?

In making a decision, you must be both realistic and optimistic—a delicate balance. At some point, you must include in any equation the limitations that exist. Restrictions such as age, education, position, knowledge, ability, and finances can be bent but not ignored.

Failure is always a possibility, but it is also a learning opportunity that should be recognized as such. Author Lloyd Morris points out: "Life constantly yields us second chances and it is in grasping them that we put our previous failures to creative use. Since we learn by doing, we succeed only by having at some time failed." The more inventive the person, the more he or she realizes this. At one point, when Thomas Edison had conducted twenty thousand unsuccessful experiments to find a substitute for lead in manufacturing storage batteries, a reporter asked him if he was "discouraged by all this waste of effort." Edison shot right back: "Waste? Nothing is wasted. I've found twenty thousand things that don't work."

In any decision, the element of personal responsibility needs to be taken into account. No person is an island. As far as can be known, the consequences—good and bad—must be weighed, for it is by their fruits that you can really know your decisions.

There is consolation in the process of decision making in the realization that no one is alone at the point of choice. There is a source of wisdom outside humankind, a source that can be tapped in prayer, as it was by Solomon: "Give your servant a heart to understand how to discern between good and evil" (1 Kings 3:9, JB).

When the time comes for an important decision, a useful road map to follow contains six basic steps:

1. *Select the goal.* After studying the situation and the facts carefully, zero in on the key question. Identify what is important and what is insignificant, what the major issues are, what is at stake. "I learned long ago," says management consultant Peter Drucker, "that the most serious mistakes are not being made as a result of wrong answers. The truly dangerous thing is asking the wrong question."

2. *Explore courses of action.* You can only be sure that you are reaching for the best choice if you free yourself from old ruts and leave yourself open to a wide range of alternatives. An explorer and searcher is geared to change, to pushing back boundaries, to blazing fresh trails. No one discovers new territory by staying in a safe, comfortable camp. Leave your "base camp." Shake loose from fixed thought-patterns. The reward may be discovery of fresh possibilities for attaining your goal.

3. *Deepen your knowledge.* Read, research, and discuss. Turn to knowledgeable sources in print and in person. Talk to others, not only over the back fence, but to those from whom you can really learn. While decision making is ultimately a solitary business, the preliminaries are best shared. "All the preparatory steps," notes a corporate executive, "must be shared to the widest extent that time and circumstance permit."

4. *Weigh the possibilities.* Examine and evaluate the choices open to you. Consider the consequences. List their advantages and disadvantages. Examine your motives for favoring a particular option, and be sure that you are not "wishing" your way to a choice. Don't let what you hope will happen cloud what you expect will happen.

5. *Let your decision brew.* Decisions emerge. Choices evolve. They only seem to strike like lightning, for even when we are not aware of the decision-making process, it goes on. Of course, deadlines often dictate the timetable for making a decision, but a wise middle course moves between rushing to judgment and avoiding a decision. When possible, a period of studying, checking, and weighing is advisable. Even putting aside a decision for a reasonable period of time helps a creative process of decision making to develop. "Sleeping on it" often helps. The architect Le Corbusier has compared the birth of a project to the birth of a child: "There's a long period of gestation . . . a lot of work in the subconscious before I make the first sketch. That lasts for months. One fine morning the project has taken form without my knowing it."

6. *Choose.* Either you choose for yourself or time, circumstances, and others will dictate a choice—directly or indirectly. Even not choosing is a form of choice. But for the examined and fulfilling life, choice is essential. It is facing the reality that living is a risk. Every undertaking in life has its uncertainties.

Face the possibility that the decision you make may turn out badly and that you will have to live with the results. You may be able to revoke a wrong decision and try again, but you cannot afford to let fear of the unknown paralyze you. Consider the epitaph placed on the tombstone of a Greek sailor shipwrecked on the coast of Asia Minor two thousand years ago: "Fear not to set sail. Ships other than ours have weathered the gale."

As with any skill, decision making lends itself to examination and inventory. To assess yourself consider these questions:

Am I alert to signs pointing to the need for a decision?

Do I make quiet time for sorting things out?

Do I face difficult decisions head-on?

Do I act, rather than drift and "let things happen"?

Do I keep up with small decisions to avoid being overwhelmed by them?

Do I set priorities?

Do I review long-standing decisions to see if they are still valid?

Do I do my own thinking, or do I just follow what the last (or most insistent) advice-giver says?

Do I try to have a back-up plan?

Do I take the time for careful consideration when needed?

Can I sense when to make a quick decision?

Do I face the fact that "the buck stops here"?

Do I see a possible opportunity in every crisis?

Inevitably, choosing involves you with others. The decisions of others, in turn, involve them with you, creating two-way traffic that demands mutual confidence and clear communications if damaging collisions are to be avoided. Above all, develop a positive attitude toward decision making, as expressed in the following Christopher prayer:

"Yes." "No." "Go." "Stay."
I seem to be always at some kind of crossroads, Lord.
I start down one road. And it forks. Or I find out I took a wrong turn and have to go back and start again.

Why so many decisions, Lord? Why so few maps or signposts?

I know. My life is unique, uncharted. It's a path no one has ever taken, so there's no travel guide.

A long time ago, You told Abram:

"Go into the land that I will show you."

You tell every child born into this world the same thing. You show us the way in the people, circumstances, and events of everyday life. And every decision we make is a step on that journey of faith—faith in You and faith in ourselves because You have made us.

Guide our feet in the right paths, Lord. Amen.

‹ 8 ›

Government Is Your Business

On the first Tuesday after the first Monday in November, when all citizens can change from spectators to decision makers, something special takes place for everyone. Power is turned over to individuals who will carry on the work of government. They get the power to raise taxes, change traffic signs, send travelers to the moon, authorize a new school gym, build bigger bombs. Wherever you turn, you face the consequences of election day decisions—for better or worse, in sickness and health, in season and out.

Unfortunately, not everyone actively participates in making voting decisions. But those who do can rightly feel they are taking part directly in working out the problems and challenges that face society. Notwithstanding all the fashionable talk that puts down politicians, what voters do is select individuals to be servants of the people. Both politicians and voters tend to forget that elected officials are literally being hired to do the jobs that individual citizens do not have the time—and sometimes the skills—to do themselves.

All sorts of advice has been given on the importance of voting decisions. The personal responsibility was particularly well stated as far back as 1748 by John Wesley, the English evangelical preacher and founder of Methodism: "Act as if the whole election depended on your single vote, and as if the whole Parliament (and therein the whole nation) on that single person whom you now choose to be a member of it."

After each U.S. presidential election, political pundits demonstrate how a few votes strategically shifted here and there would have changed the outcome. In the 1976 presidential election, it was noted that if only thirty thousand strategically placed votes out of eighty million had been cast differently, the outcome would have been reversed.

Not long ago, in the town of Clyde Hill, Washington, the election of the mayor had to be settled by the toss of a coin. Each of two candidates had received 576 votes and faced the state requirement for picking the winner.

"It's ridiculous to decide an elective office this way," fumed the incumbent as he and his opponent waited for a county official to make the toss.

The challenger was philosophical, calling it "the least offensive method." As it turned out, he won the toss.

But a coin didn't really decide that election. The nonvoters did, for if only one more person had voted, there would have been no tie.

Ogden Nash, one of the country's best-known humorous poets, has called such nonvoters "un-citizens in citizens' clothing." In "Election Day Is a Holiday," he ends by versifying:

> They attempt to justify their negligence
> On the grounds that no candidate appeals
>   to people of their intelligence,
> But I am quite sure that if Abraham Lincoln
>   (Rep.) ran against Thomas Jefferson (Dem.)
> Neither man would be appealing enough to
>   squeeze a vote out of them.

Unfortunately, too many citizens count themselves out of the November decision-making process on the local, state, and national levels. It is not a pretty statistical picture:

Only 64 percent of the eligible voters went to the polls in 1960.

In the presidential elections of both 1972 and 1975, the proportion was down to about 55 percent.

In the nonpresidential election year of 1974, a mere 36 percent voted.

All talk about participating in the political process boils down to the basic proposition expressed in *The Federalist.* In the essays that set forth the principles on which the U.S. Constitution is based, there is no question about the essential role of public participation. The people are called "the only legitimate fountain of power." From them, "the constitutional charter . . . is derived." For good measure, there are the words of Thomas Jefferson: "I know of no safer depository of the ultimate power of society but the people themselves."

Disillusionment, cynicism, a sense of powerlessness, and just plain indifference are familiar excuses as many Americans have counted themselves out of the political process. Some even argue that refusing to vote is a way of registering dissatisfaction with how politicians have conducted themselves. Others claim that staying home is more honest than casting an uninformed or thoughtless vote. Yet those who don't vote do more than count themselves out:

Nonvoters decrease the pressure that can be put on political parties to formulate platforms that truly reflect issues important to the average citizen.

Nonvoters encourage power brokers to retain control of party machinery, and they discourage men and women with new ideas and sound plans for change from trying to "buck the system."

Nonvoters allow crucial domestic and international issues to be settled by a select few, rather than subject them to the acid test of popular debate.

Nonvoters fail to keep political leaders answerable to the people, giving rise to more opportunities to exploit and manipulate the public.

In the governmental marketplace, politicians are people too. They are individuals who want to succeed, earn respect, solve problems, and face challenges. They also want to be leaders, which means they always look over their shoulders to see who is following. That is how and why the citizen as participant can make a difference.

Participation, of course, should begin long before election day. To get the most out of the political process, citizens make their voices heard in the primaries—when an individual vote counts even more than on general election day. Because primaries usually draw far fewer voters than elections, those who do turn out carry extra weight.

And before that, there is participation in political organizations. This can involve the major parties or groups that act as watchdogs and activists in influencing the actions of political parties and elected officials. Ralph Nader, for one, has inspired the formation of public citizen groups, building on this basic plank: "There can be no daily democracy without daily citizenship. If we do not exercise our civic rights, who will? If we do not perform our civic duties, who can? The fiber of a just society in pursuit of happiness is a thinking, active citizenry. That means you."

Conscientious and conscious citizenship involves a host of issues. It doesn't make sense to throw up your hands and say it is too much to consider, not when you are the one involved and you are the one affected. More than that, each person of faith feels a responsibility for what happens all around; there is no way to avoid that involvement. Consider these recurring issues, and decide how you stand. Then find out how political leaders and elected officials stand on them:

Detente. When does the effort to relax tensions between East and West become weakness in standing up for national principles and human priorities?

Unemployment. Do you favor spending billions to bring down the unemployment rate to 3 or 4 percent? Or do you agree with those who claim that keeping the lid on inflation may mean—at least for a while—no jobs for millions of Americans who are willing and able to work?

Inflation. Why did something for which you paid $1.00 in 1966 cost $1.74 ten years later? What do you want your government to do about it?

Business and labor. Do business and labor have too much influence with politicians and government officials? Where does this leave the average citizen?

Medical care. What are your views on national health insurance? What do proponents of the various plans say about costs, coverage, and possible abuses? How do they propose to eliminate profiteering, red tape, and inequities?

Food. Do you want your government to use food the way the oil-producing countries have used petroleum—as a bargaining weapon? What is America's obligation to the hungry of the world? What about agribusiness and the continuing decline in small family farms?

How should the U.S. government face the harsh realities of global food production? What about the life-and-death challenge of food distribution in a world where five hundred thousand human beings in the less-developed nations are dying of starvation each year? These countries are caught in a tightening vise: they are not agriculturally self-sufficient, do not earn enough money to import needed food, or have populations that are growing faster than food resources.

In face of these facts, a number of experts claim that our planet can feed at least three times its present population. "I am satisfied the world can feed whatever number of people there are going to be for the balance of this century," stated Dr. John Hannah, head of the World Food Council set up by the World

Food Conference in Rome during the fall of 1974. "It isn't going to be easy," he stressed, "but it can be done."

Environment. Resources are limited; energy is continuously becoming more expensive. Meanwhile, some environmental measures are blamed for closing down factories and costing workers their jobs. The issues of survival for Spaceship Earth are no longer distant. They are as visible as the polluted river almost at your doorstep, as discomfiting as smog, and as dangerous as threats to health. "Reason," argues Lutheran theologian Joseph Sittler, "says that destroying clean air is impractical. Faith ought to say it is blasphemous."

Like it or not, humankind is on the same passenger craft. Years before an astronaut looked down from a moon orbit and described the earth as a solitary object, "a grand oasis in the big vastness of space," Ambassador Adlai Stevenson made the point in his last speech to the United Nations: "We travel together, passengers on a little spaceship, dependent on its vulnerable resources of air and soil; all committed for our safety to its security and peace; preserved from annihilation only by the care, the work, and, I will say, the love we give our fragile craft."

Taxes. Government functions on all levels because of taxes. In fact, during the first months of every year—122 days—the average taxpayer works entirely to pay local, state, and federal taxes. Is government spending out of control? Do you agree with the priorities in local, state, and federal budgets? Do you know what those priorities are? Take, for example, the average amount of federal taxes paid in fiscal 1973 by each U.S. household— $3,227. This includes income tax, Social Security, excises (for example, telephone and gasoline), and business taxes passed along to consumers. According to the Tax Foundation, Inc., this is how those federal tax revenues were allocated:

Health & Welfare	$1,150
(includes social insurance)	
National Defense	1,026
Interest on Federal Debt	277

Veterans' Benefits & Services	154
Commerce & Transportation	151
Education & Manpower Training	148
General Government	138
Agriculture & Agricultural Resources	90
Community Development & Housing	64
International Affairs & Finance	50
Space Research & Technology	42
Natural Resources	32
Special Allowances	17
(Undistributed Adjustments—Intragovernmental)	−113
	$3,227

Is too much of your money being taxed? Is too much going into one category and too little into others? Your lively concern and that of millions of others can change the balance. You, as decision maker, have the right and responsibility to scrutinize those you vote for and elect. A scrutiny built out of crucial questions tests leaders before and after their election. The following questions suggest the information that politicians can be asked to supply in order to win and keep your support:

Do they favor ambitious spending programs without indicating how they will be paid for?

Do they suggest spending priorities that are in keeping with real needs and basic ideals?

Do they limit themselves to attacking opponents without explaining issues or offering specific plans?

Do they use legitimate concerns over crime and inflation to play on fears rather than to present constructive recommendations?

Are they willing to debate issues and opponents?

Do they advocate a responsible foreign policy that respects the sovereignty of all nations, cooperates with allies, and deals in honest negotiation with adversaries?

In making demands of politicians, you must also be realistic, for a politician does not thrive (or survive) by drawing only on abstract ideals. Politicians must confront others who have differ-ent opinions and different conclusions based on similar facts. They must work with others who represent different constituen-cies and have different priorities. This does not mean "selling out." It means learning what is possible and attainable and work-ing for it. When stubborn meets stubborn, there is an impasse and nothing happens.

When Senator George Aiken of Vermont retired after a long political career, he ended on a note of candor: "During the thirty-four years of my tenure as a U.S. senator, I have committed many sins." He was referring to compromises he had made in order to get bills passed into law, laws that he later regretted not oppos-ing. But politics is that way. It calls for decisions now, rather than later, and on the basis of limited information. Often, by the time all the information comes in, any action is pointless.

On the floor of Congress—or in a state legislature or town council—things are seldom as clear and simple as they may seem in a political science classroom or in a political pundit's column. Politics—the art of compromise and the art of the possible—is not cut-and-dried. It involves loose ends and horse trading. Part of its essence is making deals among vested interests and power blocs, trading support for support, matching arguments, and seeing another's point of view. In short, politics is filled with less-than-ideal choices and decisions.

Rather than criticize officeholders from a distance, move closer to them. Perhaps even join them in the rough and tum-ble of the political arena. Then you discover how much politi-cians are like the rest of us, how much they reflect their con-stituencies.

Nor can you justify asking questions of politicians without asking yourself questions, such as the following:

1. Did you vote in the last national, state, and local election? Primary?

2. Do you know who your senators and representatives in Congress are?

3. Who is the governor of your state, your representative in the state legislature?

4. Do you know how your representatives voted on major bills?

5. Do you ever have a serious discussion of bills under consideration by your state legislature?

6. Do you know how delegates are chosen from your state for the national conventions?

7. Are you active in any organization—political, environmental, business, farm, or labor—that takes positions on public issues?

8. Are you cynical or hopeful about the political process in this country?

9. Do you know how your local government is organized and how it functions?

10. Have you recently attended meetings of your local school board or zoning board or other meetings on local issues?

The discussions about how government can be made more responsive have another side. Ask, also, how citizens can become more responsive to the needs of government. Every society is like a human body; each part has a role to play. All the parts have to work together.

St. Paul put it this way: "The whole body is fitted and joined together, every joint adding its own strength" (Eph. 4:16, JB).

What strength are you adding to the body of which you are a part? For many people, government has become a dirty word; yet everyone wants the benefits of good government. Are you willing to exert yourself, to pay the price?

That price is vigilance.

That price is support of groups working for better government.

That price is a demand that too much secrecy in government be replaced by more openness.

If you think the price is high, think of the consequences of bad government—consequences for you today and for your children tomorrow.

Political leaders are not like clocks—to be wound up at election time and left to run under their own power. They depend on feedback from their electorate for guidance on crucial votes. Sometimes leaders take the initiative in seeking that feedback; at other times it's up to the citizen to initiate the feedback.

For example, one West Virginia congressman went home on his Washington recess and got to know his constituents better by slinging hash, collecting garbage, delivering newspapers, and pumping gas. In Lynbrook, Long Island, village officials met commuters at the train station with coffee, buns, and a chance to talk about local government and local problems.

An organization like Common Cause works to make government more responsive to the needs of citizens. So do Ralph Nader's public citizen groups. Public-interest lawyers have pressed for stronger environmental safeguards on the Alaska oil pipeline and have forced disclosure of secret political campaign contributions. They have brought about more accountability to local needs when radio and TV stations periodically renew their licenses.

The spirit of the process was captured by the inimitable Benjamin Franklin after the final draft of the Constitution was agreed upon in September 1787.

"What have we got, Dr. Franklin?" a woman asked him.

"Madame," he replied, "we have a republic, if we can keep it!"

Within government itself, "whistle blowers" are an encouraging sign. In their government jobs, they have spotted and brought out into the open abuses and misuse of taxpayer money. They have brought about the departure of a cabinet official for questionable contracting practices, prevented the setting up of a vast federal computer network which could compile confidential data on every citizen, and uncovered information on Air Force contracts that had cost millions more than necessary because there was no competitive bidding.

From federal bureaucrat to town clerk, from individual citizen to national watchdog organization, all kinds of people and groups help make government responsible and responsive. The more, the better, for this sort of interaction is the best antidote to minority government. As columnist Sydney Harris has noted, "Something run by a minority is always in the interest of that minority." When people care about government, government cares about people.

Specifically:

You can read carefully the newsletters from your state and congressional representatives, and answer their questionnaires promptly.

You can follow your representatives' voting records in the daily newspaper. If they are not published, you can write and/or phone local editors to remind them of their duty to provide such information.

You can examine carefully all proposals made by national, state, and local officials—whether it is a budget proposal or a plan to rezone Main Street.

You can watch closely for reports on such issues as full disclosure of campaign spending, regulation of lobbyists, conflict-of-interest legislation, unnecessary secrecy in government, and reforms in the Congressional seniority system.

Each person must take responsibility for making government his or her business, a moral which lies at the heart of a fantasy spun by the great Russian novelist Fyodor Dostoyevsky in *The Brothers Karamazov.* The supposed time is the sixteenth century, but the lesson is contemporary.

The fantasy says that Jesus Christ returned to earth only to be arrested by the grand inquisitor, the cardinal in charge of the inquisition. He tells Jesus that his message isn't needed any more, that people want bread and security, not freedom and truth. He tells Jesus that the people have surrendered control over their lives to the grand inquisitor. In exchange, he feeds them, protects them, makes decisions for them.

The grand inquisitor was right as far as the Christian message is concerned. Jesus Christ does stand for freedom. He spoke of personal responsibility, the willingness to bear the burden of deciding yes or no—and to take the consequences.

Jesus spoke a message of liberation. He challenged believers to realize and to act on their power to be agents of God's love. He asked them to respect and encourage that same ability in others.

Dostoevsky wrote the legend of the grand inquisitor because he saw so many people choosing security rather than taking the risk of living the gospel. And he saw the churches of his time encouraging that surrender of responsibility. If he were writing today about you and me, about your church and mine, your government and mine, would the story ring true?

The answer lies with each citizen on a daily basis, not just on election day. Each individual lives out his or her response, and from many individuals comes the only responsible answer: Government is your business.

‹ 9 ›

"A Whole Lot of Good"

In a New York subway station crowded with harassed riders, a sign announced: "There's a whole lot of good in this country." The words were a reminder of the good in all of us, in every person that God has put in the world. That good needs only to be discovered, acknowledged, and translated into action.

The one who can put that good into action is *you*.

Every human being alive today is part of the history of our times. History is no mystery, no result of a magical force that strikes like lightning. History is human beings working out their destinies, not surrendering to some blind imperative.

Supreme Court Justice Felix Frankfurter said, "There is no inevitability in history—except as men make it."

To former president Harry S. Truman, who was devoted to the study of history as well as making it, "Men make history and not the other way 'round." Truman liked to point out that without leaders society stands still; progress occurs "when courageous, skillful leaders seize the opportunity to change things for the better."

Anyone who tries to make a difference is a leader, whether or not he or she enters the history books. In every period of history, individual men and women have shaped the present and the future—some for better, some for worse. In every period people need to be reminded that they are important, that at least in a small way they are making history. It might be the history of their family, neighborhood, community, or country.

When Jesus reminded his listeners, "You are the light of the world" (Matt. 5:14, RSV), he meant all of us. He told us that God's light shines on each one of us. If we let it, that light will shine through us, through our attitudes and actions. That light can push back the barriers of darkness and make life brighter and warmer for many people, including ourselves.

If you look around, you will see many opportunities to translate this message into action. There are examples in your own life and in the lives of others. With its newspaper column "What One Person Can Do," The Christophers singles out a weekly example that is published by three hundred newspapers in forty-three states. It highlights individuals who demonstrate by their lives and by their actions that one specific, particular person does count. With God's help, you too can be a force for good in a turbulent world.

Norman Cousins, editor of the *Saturday Review*, spoke from his lifelong experience of making a difference in local, national, and international affairs when he said on "Christopher Closeup": "One of the very few things in life that I have learned is that no question is more futile than: 'Can one man do anything?' One man can do everything and no man can take the responsibility for undervaluing what he may be.

"One thing he can do is to connect his convictions to those of others. You get a multiplying power as you connect those ideas to the ideas of others . . . A lot depends on what we think is important. The question therefore is not what one man can do but whether one man thinks that what he believes in is important enough to tie himself to it and to let his actions reflect those beliefs."

A review of hundreds of "What One Person Can Do" columns confirms the rich harvest from action rooted in belief and

pinpoints the various components in the process. Certain individuals do personify one particular component or other, but all
share in the total dynamic of making significant differences.

HOPE

An individual who sees something that needs changing
would not try unless he or she felt change were possible. That is
another way of describing hope, a spirit that animated one criminal court judge. In Miami, Florida, Judge Alphonso Sepe used
"creative sentencing"—"the capacity of a court to find an alternative to jail."

In certain cases, Judge Sepe sentenced offenders to community service instead of prison. In one case, a young man was
ordered to teach drawing because the judge "thought it would be
more of a crime to lock this talent up in jail because he is a born
teacher." The judge added: "When someone goes to jail, he may
get worse but he will never get better. . . . Not everyone who
commits a crime is a criminal."

Judge Sepe became convinced that sentencing ought to give
the offender "some kind of duty to perform that will enhance his
own self-respect and help to heal the community of the trauma
caused by his crime." He believed in stiff jail sentences, but he
also believed that "any judge who can believe in a severe sentence must also be able to impose leniency, mercy, understanding, and kindness."

Hope led Judge Sepe to take a chance on offenders: "Judges
don't get criticized for putting people in jail. They get criticized
when they take a chance with someone and it backfires."

PERSISTENCE

It's comparatively easy to do a hard thing for a short time,
but to do even a slightly difficult thing steadily is a serious challenge to commitment. This calls for doggedness, for persistence

of the kind demonstrated by Mrs. Donna Wolfe of Kansas City, Kansas. The mother of four set about improving the ambulance service in her city after being shocked by the death of a friend. She died in an ambulance while two drivers squabbled over who would take her to the hospital.

Mrs. Wolfe spent eight years working alone on her self-chosen project. She collected news items about similar occurrences, canvassed opinions from the people involved in ambulance service, and documented the need for regulations and training requirements. She compiled a file for future reference and then walked miles circulating petitions. She enlisted the support of hospitals, churches, and PTA groups and, finally, was asked by the mayor to chair a study committee.

As a result, changes recommended by the committee were adopted, and improvements were made that she did not believe "possible ten years before." Mrs. Wolfe found that "once city officials became aware of how bad the situation was, they took an active part in improving the service." KARE, a rescue squad staffed by paramedics, was established in the fire department, and regulations and training requirements were laid down for private ambulance companies. "Without the help of many other people in the community, none of this could have been possible," reported Mrs. Wolfe, with the kind of modesty that reflects her confidence in people.

SENSE OF THE HERE

Some people who want to bring about change indulge in grandiose plans instead of looking right on their own doorstep. They get carried away by dreams and never actually do anything. Usually, the best place to begin is where you live or work. Irving Cline, in the Queens section of New York City, did just that in his neighborhood populated by middle-class people sandwiched between an area of expensive homes and a slum.

When Mr. Cline learned that the local police precinct could purchase five thousand dollars worth of security equipment if his neighbors could raise fifteen hundred dollars, he organized a cookout and collected the money. Then he went around and persuaded his neighbors to organize a block security system. When people go on vacation, a neighborhood security system watches their homes. Another time, when the area was drenched by heavy rains, he went out and borrowed a gasoline-powered pump. Going from house to house, he pumped out flooded cellars and then gave out leaflets on where to apply for disaster relief. Next came a plan to turn empty lots into vegetable gardens.

The fifty-nine-year-old sheet-metal worker claimed that he had visited every home in his neighborhood. "I know the poor, the rich, everyone in the neighborhood," he noted. "I know my people, and when they believe something can't be done, they don't try. I do it to show them it can be done."

SENSE OF THE NOW

Once missed, the opportunity to do something may never return. To the *here* of helping must be added the *now,* the readiness to act today rather than to wait for tomorrow, a lesson personified by a Springfield, Ohio, professor, John Hitt. A professor of cell biology at Wittenberg University, he set up a successful "dial-a-prof" service for his students. Each of them was given an individualized project, and if any problems arose, their professor was available at any time. They just had to call him, even late at night.

Why does Professor Hitt make himself so available? "When students need help," he explained, "they need it *now.* Quite often they will be doing their projects at night and get stumped on something." Not only will he answer calls, but he will even go over to the lab to help a student.

SETTING A SPECIFIC GOAL

To want to do some generalized good for some unspecified people is usually a waste of time and energy. But if you identify the people to be helped, specify what they need, and prepare yourself to meet that need, then you can get results. That is just what Dr. Harry King, a renowned eye specialist, did.

Dr. King centered his efforts on the International Eye Foundation, a nonprofit organization that encourages individuals to donate their eyes so others may see. In the late 1930s, Dr. King had been struck by the fact that 80 percent of the lepers he treated in Borneo had eye diseases. As his skill and reputation grew, Dr. King became chief of the Eye Department and Research at Walter Reed Hospital in Washington, D.C., where his patients included presidents Truman and Eisenhower.

But Dr. King was not interested in limiting his services to the "big people." He wanted to treat people everywhere, preferring "the masses to the classes." To further his aim, he started the eye foundation in 1961, not only for eye donors, but to train doctors in underdeveloped countries where eye diseases are rampant.

TAPPING SKILLS OF OTHERS

Instead of bemoaning the apparent fact that others lack "what it takes," look closer. You will find strength, beauty, and power in others, and you will find the personal resources to perform wonders. Cultivate the gift of tapping the skills of others. That's what Arthur Mitchell did in founding the Dance Theatre of Harlem.

Mr. Mitchell, the first black dancer to appear in classical ballet in this country, literally stopped in his tracks while on the way to Brazil. En route to the airport, he heard the news that Dr. Martin Luther King, Jr., had been assassinated. Instead of proceeding to Brazil where the State Department was sending him to help form a national dance company, he asked himself: "Why should I be going to Brazil to do this when there are so many problems in America?" He answered his own question: "Get out there and do something and start utilizing the expertise you have."

The first step was taken in a garage at St. Nicholas Avenue and 141st Street in New York City's Harlem. The door was open to anyone who walked in to study dance. It started with thirty and increased to four hundred by the end of the summer of 1968. Since then, thousands of youngsters and adults have been a part of the Harlem school. They have brought forth untapped abilities, enjoyed the beauty of the dance, and have toured the United States, Europe, and the Caribbean. "If we all remember," says Arthur Mitchell, "to utilize whatever we have in a constructive way to make better humans rather than just performers, it would be a much better world."

FEELING FOR THOSE IN NEED

Time and again, those who help others reveal an almost poetic feeling for those in need. That sensitivity does not necessarily come out in words, but it is there in what they do and how they do it. Nor is it an old-fashioned, out-dated feeling. It is still here on New York's Lower East Side where the work of Dorothy Day shines forth.

During the depths of the Great Depression, she joined a middle-aged French peasant named Peter Maurin in setting up a soup kitchen for the homeless. They saw this as literally carrying out Jesus' words: "I was hungry and you gave me food" (Matt. 25:35, RSV). They also distributed cast-off clothing to men and women who would otherwise have had to spend cold winter months coatless and shivering. The group that formed about them became known as the Catholic Worker movement, and it still provides food and clothing.

In her midseventies, gray-haired Dorothy Day—her face lined with the years—still radiates the compassion that made her a symbol of the helping hand and heart. "God can take the loaves and fishes, if that is all we have, and multiply them," she reminds everyone. "But the thing is to want to give all."

RESILIENCY

Over and beyond persisting is the refusal to let setbacks be anything but temporary. The persistent person goes on consistently and effectively; someone who has been knocked down can go farther. He or she can get up and start again. The crushing blow can be physical or mental or some event. When such people have a religious commitment, they generally turn to God as the great power in their lives. Often, they then become even more effective in striving toward their goals. As Rose Regan points out, "God does things in mysterious ways."

A widow who had raised two children on her nurse's salary, Rose Regan was stricken at age fifty-five with phlebitis. A blood clot reached her spine, and she became paralyzed from the waist down. She had to learn "a whole new way of living." For Rose Regan, the tragedy became a challenge rather than a defeat.

During a year's intensive struggle with the disease, she spent months at a rehabilitation institute, learning to get into her wheelchair by sliding out of bed on a board, learning how to bathe and dress herself, learning how to drive a car. "It was the hardest work of my life," she admits. "A lot of the time I wanted to throw the sponge in. That's normal. I felt I was given a second chance to live."

And she took that opportunity, returning to her post as assistant director of nursing at Christian Health Care Center in Wyckoff, New Jersey. Patients have gained inspiration from seeing a nurse go about her rounds in a wheelchair. "I can't do all I used to be able to," Nurse Regan reports, "but I think it made a better nurse out of me."

DEVELOPING KNOW-HOW

"Do gooders" are dismissed as cranks when they don't develop the skills necessary to bring about improvements. Doing good requires knowing how. If you don't know how, then it becomes necessary to learn, a lesson applied by a young Peace Corpsman, Ned Seligman. While working in West Africa, he ran up against the drought-stricken plight of Upper Volta villagers, and he tried to help.

Toward the end of his three-year extended tour in Upper Volta, he responded to a request by villagers and helped them shore up an old French dam to provide much-needed water. A few months later the dam collapsed because of improper construction. He became determined to discover the best methods of dam-building. So he went home to learn and to raise money.

Ned Seligman studied water development in Israel and obtained funds from foundations and from the U.S. government. He then went back to West Africa, armed with funds and know-how as a worker for Catholic Relief Services. "At home," he comments, "you keep hearing that these people have no concept of the future, and that's what keeps them poor. These people wouldn't be doing all this work if they didn't think of the future."

SENSE OF VISION

Those who work to bring about changes are able to see even in darkest circumstances how improvements are possible if the right kind of effort is made. They can see beyond inconsistencies, human frailty, and fearsome injustice to the goal that beckons them. The constant presence of that goal carries them on and sets them apart from others who do not make a difference.

Dave Gagne's vision encompassed all the starving people in the world. So he left his comfortable life and job in Minneapolis to work as a fifty-dollar-a-week director for AMOS (Alliance to Move Our Society). He actually found life easier with no car and fewer possessions, even in the upper-middle-class community of Wellesley, Massachusetts, where he went to spread concern for the world's hungry. "It's a more human way to live in this commuting, consuming community," he reports.

He is not satisfied with asking people to give money; he wants them to share his vision. He spurred a thousand people in Wellesley to join in a nationwide fast day in order to send the food money they saved for long-term development programs for the world's poor. "It's easy for people in Wellesley to write out a check for world hunger and not do anything personally," he points out. "People everywhere are starving, a fast requires us to think about that on a personal level."

David Gagne, Rose Regan, Ned Seligman, and all the others singled out are not supermen or superwomen. The greatness of their example is its everydayness. They are like all of us. The way they began was in finding something within themselves that could be nurtured and could grow; then they reached out to touch the lives of others. It's important that we don't try to glorify them. They are individuals with frustrations, limitations, ups and downs. They win and they lose, they fail and they succeed, but they go on. They feel a sense of responsibility to others and the compelling desire to share the benefits they have received from the Lord.

What they are is very human, something that is summed up by these words:

> I am only one, but I am one.
> I can't do everything, but I can do something.
> What I can do, by the grace of God, I will do.

⊰ 10 ⊱

Making a Difference

An important test of Christianity or any other system of beliefs is whether it calls upon you to live as a responsible and responsive adult. If you blindly accept what others say, then you remain in a childish state—no matter how true the sayings and the teachings. That stands in the way of growing personally, assuming responsibility, and making a difference.

So the questions to ask yourself are: Am I growing? Do I know myself better than I did last week, last month, last year? What am I doing about it? Am I taking responsibility for my life? Am I willing to say, Here I stand and I will accept the consequences of my decisions? Am I acting on my commitment to love my neighbor as myself?

There is so much talk of love, which is certainly the driving force in personal relationships. It is literally what makes the world go round. Even when it is expressed poorly, love attracts and moves people as nothing else does. But love can be empty words without meaning unless it is tested. Then it becomes strong and valuable in the lives of men and women.

You have here a framework on which to build your life. It is linked to happiness (though there is no absolute happiness in this world). Knowing yourself, taking responsibility, and acting out of love create a sense of inner harmony, contentment. It's popularly called happiness, which is achieved not as an end in itself but as the result of how you live.

Begin with knowing yourself. Unless you respond to the fascinating challenge of getting to know who you are and who you are not, then there is no basis for knowing anyone else. You cannot give what you do not possess, and you really possess only what you are within.

The ancient Greeks left a dramatic reminder of this foundation for human life. If you climb Mount Parnassus in Greece, you will reach the ruins of the twenty-five-hundred-year-old temple to Apollo at Delphi. It sits on a rocky crag one thousand feet above a fertile plain. Inscribed in the timeless marble of the temple are two words that hold deep meaning for every person: Know Thyself.

By going inside yourself and by getting in touch with your inner resources, you get to know yourself. Instead of being constantly busy, sit still and discover what is inside you. Create a quiet peace in your daily life, removed from everyday busyness. Give yourself the chance to concentrate on what is going on inside you. Get in close touch with what you think, feel, and believe.

When Erich Fromm, the psychoanalyst, was asked for a practical solution to the problems of living, he answered: "Quietness. The experience of stillness. You have to stop in order to change direction."

Jesus put it this way: "You must come away to some lonely place all by yourselves and rest for a while" (Mark 6:31, JB)

It sounds paradoxical to talk of standing aside and resting in order to be more active. But unless you fill yourself with the beauty and wonder of God's creation and the awareness of your own living self, you really have nothing to offer. Unless you find yourself, you will be lost in your surroundings and unable to lead either yourself or others.

Today people are becoming more aware of the importance

of quiet reflection. There is growing recognition that the inner as well as the outer world needs care and attention. Lawrence Le Shan, a psychologist who has written *How to Meditate*, described this trend on "Christopher Closeup":

> For three hundred years now, we've been trying to save ourselves through dealing with the outside world, learning how to manipulate reality, and it's been wonderful. . . . But we recognize now that it isn't enough. It isn't saving us. We can't stop hurting each other; we're turning our planet into an unworkable garbage pit. We recognize this more and more. . . . We're learning that we have to look inside. To really be complete, you have to deal effectively with both the outside world and the inside world. Meditation is one attempt to do this.

Meditation has entered the lives of more and more people as a way of getting in touch with themselves. It involves paying attention and concentrating on the self, getting in touch with the self—on a regular basis. Le Shan advises going into the quiet place inside yourself with the attitude of the gardener rather than the mechanic:

The mechanic tries to readjust, fix up, change. Looking at nature, the mechanic wants to make it over.

The gardener sees and accepts, takes pleasure in what is there, is in harmony with what nature produces.

Meditation as a process which "stills" the mind can open you to a sense of your self and of God's universe. It seeks to stop the constant chattering that goes on inside each person by focusing attention, by clearing the mind, by getting free of words, words, words. Unfortunately, too much mystery and mystique—even commercialism—surround an ancient practice that is a hallmark of religions East and West. In "Look Inside," one of the Christophers *News Notes*, meditation is summed up as a kind of quiet reflection you do when you are alone. It involves a regular time each day (for ten or fifteen minutes), a suitable quiet place, a restful, upright posture, and an attitude of openness.

Various techniques are used to still the mind: Concentrate on breathing by counting each exhalation from one to ten, then repeating the count; listen to some quiet music, bringing the mind back to the sounds each time it strays; repetition of a single word, phrase or prayer; reading a short Scripture passage, then remaining silent as its meaning fills your consciousness.

The late Alan Watts, a compelling interpreter of Eastern religions in the West, has a description of simple eloquence: "Simply sit down, close your eyes, and listen to all sounds that may be going on—without trying to name or identify them. Listen as you would to music. If you find that verbal thinking will not drop away, don't attempt to stop it by force of willpower. Just keep your tongue relaxed, floating easily in the lower jaw, and listen to your thoughts as if they were birds chattering outside—mere noise in the skull—and they will eventually subside of themselves, as a turbulent and muddy pool will become calm and clear if left alone."

Meditation is filling the daily lives of business executives, students, scientists, housewives, office workers. Researchers have confirmed that meditation has a healthful effect on the body as well as on the inner self.

The response to meditation is evident among new sects and movements that are attracting many followers, much to the dismay of many established religious leaders. Perhaps there is a lesson that the churches can learn in being reminded of the spiritual dimension that can be lost in social activism.

In Japan, a Jesuit priest at Sophia University, William Johnston, describes the way young people flock to a place he runs so that they can "come together regularly for this kind of contemplation." Some are fervent Christians, but others have no faith and call themselves atheists. "Yet," he reports, "they are looking for something not clearly defined; and this meditation does, I believe, lead them to discover God—not the anthropomorphic God they have rejected but the immense Being in whom we live, move, and are."

In Connecticut, the vice-president of a manufacturing company described the changes that daily meditation brought into his life: "I'm happier. I think more clearly and work more efficiently. I find myself more involved in helping other people. I've learned to deal with stress, and at the end of the day I have more energy left for my family life."

In addition to daily meditation time, try to take short "meditation breaks," even if only for fifteen or twenty seconds. They can be refreshing and stimulating.

Before going to sleep, take a "bird's eye" review of the day. Check to what extent any insights arising out of meditation have shaped your day and influenced your life.

A daily journal also helps to deepen your inner life. Even a line or two a day gives you a chance to review this week or last week or last month. Put down your inner thoughts, not to show them to anyone but for your own reflection. You will find yourself noticing recurring patterns and enduring attitudes. The result can be a fruitful dialogue with your own self and exciting discoveries.

So look inside. You are likely to discover more about yourself and about your relation to the God who sustains you. Out of your inner reaches will come the source and inspiration for action. Meditation without action is like a fruit tree with leaves only; yet the leaves are important because they make the fruit possible. Jesus may have had something like this in mind when he said, "A man's words flow out of what fills his heart" (Luke 6:45, JB).

As long as you are only repeating what someone says, you are not taking it to heart. The fruit of meditation in action involves responsibility. Jesus drove home this lesson when Peter and his brother Andrew first met Jesus and started following him. He turned right around and addressed a very blunt question to them: "*What* do you want?" He wasn't going to let them off easily. He wanted them to take personal responsibility, not to follow him blindly.

Peter and Andrew may not have known exactly what they wanted, but they wanted more than they saw around them. When they asked Jesus where he lived, he answered, "Come and see." With his answers, Jesus was offering them uncertainty and the challenge that they find out for themselves.

That question, What do you want? still confronts all of us. And it has no easy answers, a point that Jesus made when he was asked for answers and instead confounded the simplicity seekers. To the question of ending wars and the threat of nuclear annihilation, Jesus says: "All who take the sword will perish by the sword" (Matt. 26:52, RSV). Of the fight against poverty, Jesus says: "Go and sell what thou hast, and give it to the poor, . . . and come and follow me" (Matt. 19:21, KJV). Of safer streets and prison reform, he says: "I was . . . in prison and you came to see me" (Matt. 25:36, JB). Of the feeling that nobody cares about you, he says: "The hairs of your head are all numbered" (Matt. 10:30). Of worries about civilization and its distracting affluence, he reminds us that evil "never comes out except by prayer and fasting" (Matt. 17:21, RSV).

The theologian Avery Dulles has noted that "the life of faith consists in constant probing." He points out that "easy answers are not faith, and faith is no answer except to the man who questions deeply." Jesus used the technique of answering questions with questions to emphasize that there are no easy answers. It was a technique rooted in the Old Testament, and it called for active seeking rather than passive accepting.

The very process of probing and of seeking answers is part of taking responsibility for yourself and for your actions. In fact, the search itself involves taking action, *doing.* Then answers have personal meaning; they become yours.

When Jesus was asked, "Who is my neighbour?" he told a story that led to a question, the story of the Good Samaritan. A man who was robbed and left for dead by the roadside was ignored by two people who could be expected to help him, but an outsider became the agent of God's love and healing. "Which of these three, do you think, proved neighbor to the man who fell among robbers?" Jesus asked (Luke 10:36, RSV).

Clearly, a neighbor is someone you experience as caring for you, not someone put in a certain category or given a label. A neighbor is someone who responds to your needs. It means something to have a neighbor. It means everything to be one.

To live a life that is fully human means to care—to accept responsibility for the world as you find it, not as you would like it to be. It means seeing fellow human beings as your neighbors. What you are is revealed by what you do, not by what you call yourself. To call oneself a believer is not enough. What you *do* is the test of whether you believe—and are—what you say.

The questions that Jesus addressed to his followers are still being asked today. They are not theoretical or academic; they are not even theological. They come to us through people in need. Everything depends on how each individual answers those questions.

What propels answers into action is love. It is the desire to give something of yourself to others and to receive in return, but many things are called love that are not. One way to tell the difference is in whether it melts away.

It is hardly possible to surpass the description of love in 1 Corinthians 13:4–8: "Love is patient and kind; love is not jealous or boastful; it is not arrogant or rude. Love does not insist on its own way; it is not irritable or resentful; it does not rejoice at wrong, but rejoices in the right. Love bears all things, believes all things, hopes all things, endures all things. Love never ends" (RSV).

The test of love—of seriousness of purpose—comes when the fires of youth or zeal are burning low, when it's an effort just to get up in the morning, when nobody is looking and nobody seems to care. The ultimate example came centuries ago when someone literally fulfilled his own words: "Greater love has no man than this, that a man lay down his life for his friends" (John 12:13, RSV).

This way of life is not necessarily going to provide immediate payoffs. It may seem that nothing happens, particularly when you are tempted to look up at the "scoreboard" to see results posted on the spot. But little by little, almost imperceptibly, the impact will be felt in your life. Economically or physically the results may not show, but those who live with a persevering sense of self and of responsibility to others begin to change.

This change is often referred to as happiness. It is neither perfect nor static. It comes and goes. It gets more or less intense. It's not something that you can set as a goal. You can't sit down and say: "I'm going to be happy—even if it makes me miserable." You can't capture happiness. The best thing to do is live the kind of life that over the centuries has brought happiness to people.

Jesus showed the way in the kind of life he lived. Then happiness catches you. It was summed up by Jesus in St. Matthew's Gospel. Each of eight sayings begin with "Happy are they . . ." These sayings are called the Beatitudes.

Take, for example, "How happy are the poor in spirit; theirs is the kingdom of heaven" (Matt. 5:3, JB). A milk-truck driver in Massachusetts provided a modern parable of "the poor in spirit" that is clearer than any theological treatise. He won a million dollars in the state lottery, which meant an income of fifty thousand dollars a year for twenty years. All he had to do was sit back and cash the checks, but this father of three had no intention of quitting his job or changing his life. "We were very happy before all this happened to us," he said. "We're not going to let a lot of money spoil that for any of us."

The milk-truck driver knew what billionaire J. Paul Getty belatedly admitted amidst his fortune of two to four billion dollars. Getty, one of the world's richest men, often said he would rather be a California beachcomber than a billionaire. His money was a high wall cutting him off from the simple beauties of life.

In his nineties he was still working ten hours a day, watching over his riches.

Yet Getty admitted that what he really wanted was a happy marriage to look back on instead of five divorces. He readily acknowledged that his money could not buy happiness. Instead, he observed: "It has some connection with unhappiness." This came from a billionaire who even installed a pay phone for house guests so they would not run up his telephone bill.

To be "poor in spirit" means not to depend on material things to make you happy. It is not a matter of not having or selling your color TV or sports car. It is a matter of not depending on them for happiness. It is personal liberation and freedom so that the source of your happiness is not property but people, not caring for things but caring for others.

Erich Fromm presented the challenge of freedom from things in this way: "If I am what I have—if what I have is lost, who then am I?" So the phrase "poor in spirit" says more about the way you look at possessions than the amount of the possessions themselves. It means being able to do with or do without, knowing that everything depends on God.

The other Beatitude that strikes at the core of many crises in the world today says: "Happy are those who hunger and thirst for what is right; they shall be satisfied" (Matt. 5:6, JB). This cry for justice needs to be heard urgently when:

Children in this country and overseas die of preventable diseases caused by malnutrition.

Seventy percent of the world's people get only 30 percent of the world's income.

A poor country must spend most of its foreign reserves to import food and has little left to plant next year's crop.

Thirty times as much money is spent by the world's nations on armaments as on helping the poor.

Hunger and thirst are incessant drives for the preservation

of life. Hunger and thirst for what is right, for justice, can also be a drive for each individual who cares. Maybe that hunger won't be satisfied in this life. It's not our business to know. It's our job to try, in every way possible, to see that justice is done—in personal lives, in relationships with family and neighbors, and, to whatever extent possible, in the nation and in the world.

Looking back over this book as it concludes, we may feel that we fall short of the ideals that have been held up. This is human and realistic. No one has to feel inadequate at not being superman or superwoman. Ideals are vital because they set goals to strive for. Without them, all of us would tend to slip downward instead of struggling upward. Ideals challenge you to care more about yourself and others and to respect the life God has given everyone.

Concluding a book—for readers as well as authors—is an ending in a certain way, but more importantly it is a beginning. We hope this book has provided you with useful information, introduced you to meaningful fellow humans, and given you greater confidence in yourself, your world, and your possibilities. We hope it has reminded you of your relationship to the divine being who cares about you.

The future is still a blank page that each of us must write for ourselves. You have to fill your pages. No one else can do it for you. You have certain talents, drives, abilities, feelings, and unexpressed desires that might begin to emerge after reflecting on these ideas.

Give yourself permission to follow your good instincts. First acknowledge them, then follow them farther than you might have otherwise. The obstacles, chains, and barriers that prevent you from doing what you want to do are usually self-imposed. Often, the feeling that others do not approve or will scoff holds you back. Act now, for how you live ultimately comes down to you and your Creator.

It is your life, the only one you have, and it is growing shorter with each passing day. It is filled with hopes that may have been suppressed or beset by fears. Let hope begin to predominate. Let its sunshine warm and illuminate your life.

Be glad and grateful that you are a human being living in this part of the twentieth century, with all its immense problems and unanswered questions. It is the time chosen from all eternity for you to live with the persons that are important in your life. While this may have been decided from all eternity, what only you can settle is how you are going to live out your years.

The power is in your hands to do more than you can imagine. The power will be given to you each day as it comes along. The elements are present for a life that is not only unique, but can be glorious. No one outside your immediate circle may know about it, perhaps not even they. But you will know.

If you take your own life and your own humanity seriously and learn to be at ease within yourself . . .

If you make serious efforts to develop the skills of caring, communicating, serving others . . .

If you look around and see human needs that others did not notice or did not fill . . .

If you try to fill those needs . . .

Then you will live a life in which you feel satisfied, fulfilled, happy.

Then you will ratify the fact that you are an individual unique throughout all eternity with something special to offer the world.

Then you will make a difference and verify the underlying theme of this book: *you can* still *change the world*.